Praise for *Rimonim*

"Aurora Levins Morales's poetry radiates wisdom, warmth, and fortitude. A prophetic, life-centered guide for times of tumult and struggle."
— Arielle Angel, editor-in-chief of *Jewish Currents*

"Don't you need a blessing from the grandmothers? A reconsecration of your relationship to Earth? Then you need the words of this 'fierce Latina Jew holding out a rose to Palestine.' In these poems, as always, Aurora Levins Morales reminds us that who we are has never been simple but who we are is also holy. These are the poems that invite us to act accordingly."
— Alexis Pauline Gumbs, author of *Survival Is a Promise: The Eternal Life of Audre Lorde*

"An answered prayer! A prayer itself! This book is such a glorious remedy to carry us through our days and seasons. Drawing on a lineage of revolutionary poet-prophets, Aurora Levins Morales roots into the fertile margins and weaves the liturgy we need for these times of fire and crisis. Infused with water and stone, these prayer-poems irrigate and ground us, (re)orienting and (re)organizing us to earth, to each other, to ourselves, and to what we hold sacred. Blessed are we and blessed is she for bringing forth this generous, gorgeous, much needed and desired offering."
— Dori Midnight, community care practitioner, ritual leader, and writer

"This healing, generous collection from the voice of a treasured, prophetic elder is medicine for the long haul. An abundant collection of seeds, the poems of *Rimonim* celebrate and affirm that we are interconnected, embedded in a sacred web of those who rest, rise, labor, love, sow, weave, grieve, and give. These breathtaking poems and prayers invite us to lay down our 'illusions of separation' and to know that 'each wound is full of possibility.' *Rimonim* offers so much to our multilingual, multiracial, intergenerational, diasporic Jewish communities and movements for justice. I am so grateful for this long-awaited collection and the world conjured within it. 'Bless me,' Levins Morales writes and generations will echo, 'for this is the time and I am awake.' *Que viva! Amen!*"
— Mónica Gomery, author of *Might Kindred*

"*Rimonim* is a sacred offering. Simultaneously rooted and ephemeral, sensory and transcendent, of the earth and of the spirits, this book is a gift to organizers and seekers everywhere. Aurora Levins Morales weaves together our past with our present, daring

us to imagine a future born from our most liberated dreams and desires. It's one of those 'keep this by your bedside' books that I will return to over and over again, with deep admiration and gratitude."
— Audrey Sasson, executive director of Jews for Racial & Economic Justice

"Aurora Levins Morales's liturgical work is not just poetry; it's a divine echo of comfort, legend, and ethereal beauty that resonates deeply with those in need of ethically aligned spiritual nourishment. In *Rimonim*, Levins Morales masterfully weaves her ancestral spiritual heritage with sophisticated, nuanced, and precise understanding of the most urgent calls for justice and liberation of our time. This is the poetry of a true tzaddik, whose legendary work facilitates healing and opens portals of possibility and hope, guiding us toward a more inspired, compassionate, and just future."
— April N. Baskin, founding director of Joyous Justice

"Aurora Levins Morales has provided the words we need, at a time when our pain and yearning have rendered so many of us speechless. Liturgy and lament, prose and praise, this collection represents an extraordinary exploration of the landscape of the soul. Simultaneously cosmic and intimate, Levins Morales's writing is populated with characters who live with and within you, from abuelos to garment workers to biblical matriarchs. This volume promises to be beloved in the bedroom and on the bima, and everywhere in between."
— Rabbi Michael Rothbaum, Congregation Bet Haverim

"Aurora Levins Morales has gifted us an exquisite collection of poetic prayer and prophecy that can lift our spirits, embolden us to listen to the truth of our innermost experience, and open the channel of holy connection that flows between us, our ancestors, and 'the breath of life in all things.' For those of us who already engage with Jewish liturgy, this book will change the way we pray. For those of us who struggle to recognize ourselves in Jewish liturgy, this book will make it possible for us to pray. And for all of us, whether or not we have a relationship with Jewish prayer, this book opens a window into the beauty and struggle of a life lived with integrity, clarity, and sacred connection to all that is."
— Rabbi Dev Noily, Kehilla Community Synagogue

RIMONIM

Ritual Poetry of Jewish Liberation

Aurora Levins Morales

Rimonim: Ritual Poetry of Jewish Liberation
By Aurora Levins Morales

This book was made possible through the generous support of the Opaline Fund, Anne Germanacos, Lippman Kanfer Foundation for Living Torah, and Rise Up, as well as others noted in the author's gratitudes. We are grateful for their commitment to the transformative power of creative work, and to amplifying a polyphony of voices from within and beyond the Jewish world.

Cover image by Ricardo Levins Morales
Chapter title page artwork by Maayan Alper-Swan
Book design and typesetting by Tom Haviv with Nat Brower

This book was typeset in Agmena, Alegreya, Hadassah Friedlaender, and Lapture.

First Edition
First Printing

Ayin Press
Brooklyn, New York
www.ayinpress.org
info@ayinpress.org

Published in partnership with Palabrera Press
Distributed by Publishers Group West, an Ingram brand
Printed in China

ISBN (paperback): 978-1-961814-17-2
ISBN (e-book): 978-1-961814-18-9

Library of Congress Control Number: 2024930837

Ayin Press books may be purchased at a discounted rate by wholesalers, booksellers, book clubs, schools, universities, synagogues, community organizations, and other institutions buying in bulk. For more information, please email info@ayinpress.org.

Follow us on Facebook, Instagram, or Twitter @AyinPress.

Gratitudes &

Rimonim was born out of three words from Rabbi Dev Noily of Kehilla Community Synagogue, right after I gave a Yom Kippur morning sermon: *poet in residence*. But my synagogue didn't have the money for such a post. So I reached out to the rabbis and organizational leaders who kept asking for poems they could put to use, and asked them to be my sponsors, so I could be a poet in residence to them all. The very first to say yes were the members of Jewish Voice for Peace (JVP) New Orleans. They were followed by more than a dozen other groups. Because I have had multiple head injuries since I launched this project, and because the full list of early donors vanished with the demise of my last computer, I can no longer remember everything about who helped in what ways. Synagogues who either donated directly or sponsored me in the creation of portions of this work include Kehilla in the Bay Area, Kadima in Seattle, Kol Tzedek in Philadelphia, T'chiya in Detroit and Tzedek Chicago. JVP chapters in San Francisco, Philadelphia, New York and Chicago helped in one way or another, along with chaverim in Philadelphia, Durham and New Haven, and one radical chicken and culture farm, Linke Fligl. Please forgive any omissions. People from many parts of my network, with strong representation from the Bay Area and Seattle, orchestrated a crowd fundraiser: Eden Amital, Dvora Gordon, Shifra Tobacman, Jenny Arsanow, Jake Erlich, May Ye and our dear Mads Deshazo and Sandy Bredt, now with the ancestors. This initial support allowed me to get started and led to larger grants. My heartfelt gratitude to everyone who helped, especially Claudia Horwitz of Rise Up who practically insisted I apply for a grant, and when I was very ill, let me talk my way through my application, and to my comrades at Jewish Liberation Fund who understood that poetry is part of movement building. Also the Jews of Color Initiative funded payments to BIJOCSM artists for the beautiful illustrations in this book, including the cover art. Three groups hosted me to co-create community ritual: T'chiya Synagogue with Detroit Jews for Justice; New Orleans Jewish Voice for Peace, and Tzedek Chicago with Chi-Nations Youth Council. Most of the Passover and Sukkot portions of this book were crafted in ritual practice with the members of these groups. Gratitude to the artists whose work graces these pages. Their names, bios and contact information are in the end notes.

Thank you to Jonah Aline Daniels for candlelight and to all the Rad Rabs who gathered in my father's house to talk about many things, including trauma, history and liberation. Gratitude and love to my Kehilla community where I've found and fought for home, to all my Jews of Color comrades and networks, for, you know, everything. To my students at RRC, my colleagues in the Rise Up Community of Practice, and all the radical Jewish circles within which I move, nourished and upheld. Love and gratitude to my co-counseling web, especially, for support with this book, Catalina, Tanya, Ama, Julie, Michael, Joelle, Billy, and Cherie. Gratitude to all the many of us who raise our voices, move our bodies, write our words, sing out, take stands, who refuse to let any settler-colonial project, anywhere that we live, make us accomplices to anyone else's exile, land theft, killing. I have many thought partners in all the work I do. Today I will call out the names of my brothers Ricardo and Alejandro and my dear friends April Rosenblum and Jenny Helbraun. Finally, especially, ecstatically, in such deep gratitude, I name my cherished practice of mutual Jewitchy book midwifery with Dori Midnight who over and over directed me back to what I most authentically know, and chewed on every word in this book long before they reached these pages.

Dedicated

to my great-grandmother Leah's grandmother
a woman whose name I do not know
the wife of a rabbi in the city of Kremenchuk
on the Dnieper River in Ukraine
whom Leah said "planted the revolutionary spark" in her,
a better scholar than her rabbi husband
who when she asked why she couldn't be a rabbi herself
was told it was God's law
and who stood up in temple and said,
"Your God is a man" and walked out
taking the Rabbi with her.
Seven generations later
my daughter stood on the bima
and spoke a drash against the war in Iraq.
Today I offer in her name
these poems and prayers
for all of us who have been denied voice
and took it anyway
and all those who rejoiced when we did.

Contents &

Juana Alicia

INTRODUCTION

I live on a mountain of revelation and listen to what water says as it makes its way through air and earth, through plants and animals, falling as rain, rising as fog, condensing as dew. It is the mountain itself, and the ways of my people winding through it, that teach me the necessities of this time, command me with consequence and promise. My tablets are made of leaf and feather, not stone. I listen to soil and rock, seed and worm, hawk and hummingbird. I do not need the trees, the bushes, the little flowering weeds to burst into enduring flame to hear the sacred speak.

There is fire enough in the world. The smoke of the burning Amazon, the fumes of war, the flares of chemical plants, mingled with the dust rising from slaughtered wilderness, the final exhalations of millions before their times. Wind girdles the world and we all breathe the same air filled with soot and spores, grief and seeds, pollen and aching hope. I am on a mountain of revelation and the voice I hear says what it has always said: go stammering into the world and speak, even if you're afraid, even if you feel incompetent, even if you are mocked for hoping, even if there are disappointed multitudes who want you to heal the black hole of our ancestral trauma with your words, and end all confusion. Believe me, raised as I was to reach for liberation, every day in every way, I have tried.

The only poetry, essays, stories, speeches approved by the wild ginger on the hill and the quarrelsome woodpeckers carving their hunger into the dead flamboyán are the ones I write for myself, the medicine I make for what heals *my* wounds. Those are the ones that go viral because they ring true. They are not written to please anyone. They are the rain that falls onto the page.

I am teaching my body to be rooted in the tumultuous stream, to let floods of shared pain part around me instead of thickening my veins, lodging in heart and lungs, agitating bowels and brain. I am learning to part the flood by being still and listening. I was commanded to take the alphabet and turn it into a wellspring and keep my head above water while I did it. The words I am to speak must help me stay alive, for if I am not for myself, how can I possibly be for others? As a child of revolutionaries, I learned how to be for the world, but even as we sang *There's a hole in the bucket, dear Henry, dear Henry*, no one taught me you can't haul water with a broken pail. I am teaching myself to be watertight.

Prophecy doesn't predict the future. It reveals the present and predicts its consequences, demands action toward the greater good, so the future will reflect good choices in the now. As my brother says, it opens a window into the future we dream and lets the fresh air blow through.

The original people of Northern California, where I lived most of my adult life, wove baskets so tightly made they could carry water without dripping. If I deepen my connection to everything and everyone and weave myself through it snugly enough, I will be able feel the consequences and possibilities of the world without sickening from them. I will be able to carry water in the form of words. I will not lose myself in the grief and fury of witnessing harm. So I am tending my basket in order to live a life of prophecy.

Miriam, wise woman of my father's people, said *Aren't we all prophets?* and she was smitten with leprosy and cast out into the wilderness. I like to think of her, dowsing for her personal well, gathering desert herbs, trapping small game to stew with leeks, kindling her campfires under the stars. She was sick, disabled and she lived unhoused in the wildlands at the mercy of scorpions and hyenas, but she knew her purpose even if her brother, carrying the tablets of law down from the summit, did not.

Anacaona, poet and diplomat of my mother's Indigenous people, was offered a choice by the brutal invaders of this land, as they executed caciques, healers and bohiques* for the crime of being themselves. They said if she agreed to nightly rape as a concubine, they would spare her life, and she refused what was *not* a life and was hanged. If she could not stop their wave of destruction, she would not lie down beneath it, and her choice made her a prophet. She knew her worth, if her killers did not and she knew the consequences of surrender, even when the only other option is dying. I think of her in the land of the dead, Coaybay, with a shining rope around her neck like a golden collar, waiting to be reborn. *Come now*, I whisper.

Eartha Kitt grew up in the wilderness of poverty and abandonment and sang like an angel, and one day some man with a camera pointed at her asked her was she hard to live with. *That's not for me to decide,* she said, *that's for someone who decides to live with me to decide.* The offscreen white man voice asked her would she compromise for love, wouldn't she, if a man came into her life, just compromise, and she threw back her head and laughed and said *For what? When*

---

* Caciques were political & territorial leaders; bohiques were shamanic spiritual leaders.

you fall in love, what is there to compromise about? Then the man voice, intending admonition, asked did she just fall in love with herself and she thought about it and said *Yes, I fall in love with myself and I want someone to share it with me, to share me with me*, and that is my job. To fall in love with who I am and am becoming, and with the words that rise in me, and invite you to join me. This is where the conversation begins.

A lot of people asked me to write this book, and I had to listen and then shed their needs, listen to other people's hungers for the resonances that revealed my own. I had to dowse for my perpetual well, find my own place in the margins of our sacred texts to scribble my personal siddur. I had to commit to my worth and lie down only for rest and pleasure. I had to say, *Compromise? For what?* I had to own the name of prophecy for what I do.

The poems in this book have changed over these seven years I spent writing them. I had to peel away everything I wrote for the wrong reasons and pare it all down to the necessary bone. I had to make it absolutely my own and fall in love with it. I am ready. Come share me with me.

Night & Day

EVENING PRAYER

Blessed are the tides of living that draw my body to rest and my soul to dreaming.

Let me lay the work of the world in the open hands of those still awake to the west of me, place in their palms the sickle and the spade, the needle and the shuttle, the pen and the ladle, the cell phone and the keyboard. Let me lie down in peace, as the mending of life rolls west and westward, hand to hand, village to village, through city after city, across fields and forests, deserts and oceans, moving upstream, against the planetary spin, for the dance of liberation never ceases, but keeps circling the world.

As I lie down, others rise up in a wave of intention and effort that moves in the wake of the sun, along the paths of daylight. So let my sleep be cradled in trust that others will carry what must be carried. Let my rest be unbroken by troubling thoughts or illusions of separation. Let me go down into sleep as into the arms of a beloved.

And let me rise in peace. Let me awaken to the light of a new day, and receive the work for which I was born back into my hands from those to the east of me, transformed by the many who have hammered and stitched and stirred while I slept, and whether the sun shines unveiled or is swathed in cloud, oh, radiant unruled life force of the universe, may I behold the splendor of your indwelling light, which illuminates the world.

AWAKE

There is a pink light at dawn, in spring
that signals the trees to bloom
because this is the moment for blossoming so that
there will be seeds nestled in the fruits of summer.

There are cells in the bodies of caterpillars
that wake when the worm has outgrown the cocoon
singing dissolve, unmake yourself, it's time
to become something winged, beyond your imagining.

There is a medicine in the bodies of willows
that calls forth roots from the broken twigs
and says to the cuttings, each wound is full of possibility,
let your torn edges tingle, and start again.

I am awake now to the promise of this day,
to push out buds, to be wide petalled,
to welcome pollen, set fruit. I am awake now,
to the unmaking that comes before transformation,
awake to becoming new and improbable.

I am awake now,
in all my torn and splintered glory,
ready to root into the soil and heal.

Bless me, for this is the time and I am awake.

Juana Alicia

A CALL TO PRAYER

Do not rise, do not brace your feet, calves, knees,
thighs, your whole tired selves to push
against gravity, against rest; and do not rise in spirit,
hurling yourself skyward, but instead
lie down. Sink.
Open wide your hard working hands
and let go of all striving.
Let yourself fall
gently and completely
to earth.
Go down into the holy roots of being
where your prayers spread slowly
by aquifer and mycelium,
into the common ground,
or do not spread,
and enrich the soil of
exactly where you are,
then pray.

S'FATAI TIFTACH

Ruach chai s'fatai tiftach
ufi yagid, yagid al tzedek.

Oh breath of life, come part my lips,
let justice be my song.

SH'MA

Hear all you who wrestle with life's meaning:
Ha Malchut, that which is sovereign in the universe,
unruled by king or corporation, the breath of life in all things,
the web of reciprocity, this is our one and only guide.

ASHER YATZAR

Blessed is the evolutionary dance of life, which formed the human body in perfect wisdom, made cerebellum and cortex, made the many branching nerves, the bones and their marrows, the muscles and ligaments, the red cells and the white, the myriad hormones singing their biochemical song of praise, made eyes and ears, capillaries and fingernails, the magnificent heart with its chambers, all the organs and passages, cavities and openings. Blessed is natural selection and the infinite diversity of our shapes and colors, our forms and functions, and blessed is the ability to adapt, for it is well known and obvious that each one of us is made as we should be, that even though openings close, and closures open, even though limbs grow wildly and genes mutate, even though hearts dance to different drummers, lungs labor, bones bend and break, and biochemical signals go awry, even though we age and will someday die, we are infinitely splendid as we are. Blessed are you, life force of the universe, that has made us so varied and resilient.

Roan Boucher

HANDWASHING

A Call and Response with Dori Midnight

Wash your hands like you are washing the only teacup left that your great-grandmother carried across the ocean,

like your hands are the last shard lifted from the earth that completes the shattered bowl

like you are washing the hair of a beloved who is dying

your fingers braiding ribbons of water through minutes that fall, drop by drop onto the floor, into the hush that is still breathing

Like this water is poured from a jug your best friend just carried for three miles from the spring they had to climb a mountain to reach.

and these drops we pour on our fingers are the same ones our ancestors drank as miraculous desert dew, the ones that thunder endlessly down the falls of Iguazú, the ones carried for miles on the heads of women in Kenya and Benin in five-gallon, forty-pound cans, the single tepid sip from a shared canteen in a prison camp, the wild shower scattering rainbows, the tears that brim at such beauty.

Wash your hands like it's a transfusion, and someone all the way across the city will survive the surgery now.

and this is the water of every mikvah that has ever existed, and we are blessing ourselves into the next moment of our common good.

and this is rain falling in Haiti, snow falling in the boreal forests, steam rising from the heaving salty bosom of the ocean.

Wash your hands like it's the gush of water from a womb and someone we will love forever is about to be born.

and this water we pour has danced round our planet since the very first molecules came hurtling out of the sky, clinging to celestial rock

and this water has passed in and out of all our generations, charged with memory, so that we pour the stories of a billion years across our palms.

wash your everyday skin while you count to twenty

slowly, like the seconds are heartbeats and you are in love.

like every precious thing is here

right now

in our hands

ORIGINAL INSTRUCTIONS

Praise be to the life force that grew us from seed, from single cells floating in brine, and through all the miracles of evolution made us human beings, created to live together, created to share food and water, created to carry each others' babies, created to tend and shelter each other. We praise the commandments of our true natures, to honor each other, to honor the earth and all that lives, to seek justice as plants seek the sun, not for duty but for sustenance and joy. We honor the gift of breath by living this day according to the deep commands of our creation, our original instructions.

Seven Sacreds

One of my dear people asked for seven
psalms for the days of the week, and I
tried, but they didn't work. At last I came
home to my own intimate, personal
practices of the sacred. To remembering
that in the midst of my passion for words,
I write my midrash in color and thread
and the cooking pot. My midrash is water,
herbs, garlic, flowers, indigo. Here are
seven day-to-day ways I touch the sacred.
What are yours?

One

DYEING

INDIGO

Bless the blue that blooms
as I inch the cloth
from the yellow-green swamp
of the dye bath.
Bless the chemistry of color,
how it's oxygen,
the exhalation of trees
the breathable heaven
that causes hidden molecules
to bind to fiber and become
sky, midnight, ocean.
How the folds and knots
become white constellations
fish scales, zig zags of lightening,
igniting the deep, deep blue
from which everything was born,
that stains my fingertips for days.

COCHINEAL

Conquerors imagined them to be seeds,
blossoms that became worms,
could not decipher the magic
of such a true red. Mayan weavers
covered their smiles with their hands,
gathered the tiny grey beetles
that live among the thorns of nopal.
I do not gather them.

They arrive in small bags, migrating by mail.
Their dried bodies drop into the vat
and explode into magenta.
I stand at the stove, stirring four pots.
A few drops of vinegar make crimson,
a few grains of soda make purple.
From these little insects pours
the whole spectrum
from flame to grape,
from blood to rose.

When the secret finally cracks
merchants must load their ships with cactus
to feed the precious insects
for the color they crave

and Istanbul traders turn nopal
into sabra, marking the boundaries
of Palestinian plots with the one food
of the cochinillas, the little pigs,
their grey corpses boiled
to dye the fine robes of kings,
the wool and cotton
of carpet and keffiyeh,
make fiery circles on silk
to keep me cozy through mountain nights,
fire of Mayan villages
warming my bones.

ACHIOTE

With these grains of red gold,
my archipelagan ancestors
painted their faces
the colors of rust and clay,

but in the vat, they are liquid sun
dripping from the edge of a scarf
the hem of a dress, and in the pan
they bleed orange into the oil.
This is the joy of the wild dye,
to never know if I will get sunflower
or tangerine, sunset or burnt orange.
It is the art of surprise, the blessing
of the unplanned.

Two

GARMENTS

Every garment can be a tallis.
Spirit is in the details, the stitching,
the fibers, the weave. I cut and sew,
embroider and mend, I choose the the pants
with the wide yoke, the breathable waist,
the shirt dyed like rainy-day clouds,
the one with swirls like ocean currents,
the long white linen shift.
Each one is an intention,
each one a way to enter
the day, the night, the moment.
Each one a song of ancestors, of
all my affinities: Caribbean waters,
tropical rain, spattered leaves and striped wind,
the wide legs and gathered ankles
of brown kin in hot places, the t-shirts
each one a poem, the loose tops and tunics
my storyteller's robes.
Each one is a treasured story
burnished to a high gleam by the telling:
The African pants in pea green foliage
I bought that autumn in New Orleans,
the micro-patterned purple XL dress shirt
from the general store in Glendive, Montana
snowed in, two days out of Standing Rock,
in a campground full of oil workers.
The fuchsia Irish sweater I gifted myself
for finishing a book.

I come from garment workers
tailors and dressmakers,
sweatshop and factory workers,

makers of lace and uniforms, shirtwaists,
girdles and bras. When I tie my knots,
when I take in, let out, replace elastic gone saggy
their fingers interlace with mine,
Their fingers, pierced by needles,
their knotted knuckles finally at rest
swing from gussets and hems like tzitzit.
Each buttonhole is a blessing.
Each seam is praise.

Blessed too is the spirit
that sanctifies our style,
that decks us with shattered light
and glinting buckles.

Behold, I am wrapped in my choices,
I am garbed with splendor
I drink from rivers of delight.

Three

TOSTONES

Oh, how that kitchen was filled with patriarchy
and perfectionism. Abuelo Manolín,
the embodiment of authority,
the sole possessor of the
Right Way to Do Things.
How to scramble tomatoes into eggs,
serve ice cream on top of cake,
no matter how much I protested the
sogginess. But bless
the exquisite craft of the perfect tostón,
he made me practice for hours
apron round my waist,
up on a stool to reach the stove,
until he was satisfied.

Praise the perfection of the pot,
recipes measured by handfuls
timing by breath, the rooted cook,
generations peering over her shoulders
shaking their heads, guiding the knife,
whispering advice.

They tell me to peel green plátano
under running water, to loosen the skin.
To slice it just right. Too thick, it stays raw,
too thin, it burns into chips. Pour oil
two finger joints deep and throw in a dozen cloves of garlic
that sizzle and scent the air.

Drop in the pieces. Be patient.
Let each side become tender
before you flip or scoop.

Never, never use a tostonera,
those wooden castanets
that make bulky tasteless wedges.
You need a brown paper bag
from the corner grocery store,
the bottom folded over
to protect your palm.
Paper towels to drain the grease.

Each slice takes its turn on the brown paper
a crescent of garlic on top. This
is the moment of truth.
You fold the thickest part over,
place your palm flat,
lean in, giving it your weight
and slowly slide and twist
until the plantain
is thin enough for crunch,
thick enough not to tear,
and slip the wafer of garlicky starch
into the hot pan
watch it go crisp and golden,
sacramental.

Then abuelo, his craftsman's hand
heavy on my shoulder, nods approval,
says in his voice of a bossy ghost,
así mismo mija. Así. Amen.

Four

BITTERS

In a world of sugar and salt
let us praise the bitter truth.

I fill a bowl with roots of gentian,
with turmeric and clove,
ginger and Oregon grape,
cardamom and orange peel,
angelica and myrrh.

Stand at the counter,
sifting roots and seeds
barks and gums
into crystal clear white rum,
an incantation for my liver,
for the flow of bile,
for the power to digest.

Weeks later the rum is dark
as a swamp at midnight,
bitterness as good as an honest word,
as apology heartfelt
as naming the injury
and cleaning the wound.

There is nothing wrong with honey
with the handful of salt,
with vinegar and chilis
that pucker and burn,
but bitter is a cleansing wind,
a cold drenching seawater spray

the first thin sliver of light
after the new moon,
the harsh husk
from which the new leaf
springs.

Five

TEA

Tea was my mother's gift,
the brown pot swirled with boiling water
the shriveled black leaves,
pinched between five fingers
out of imported chests, fragrant with tannins
and the jasmine she picked and dried.

Insomniac nights
she paced the hall with steaming mugs,
and Sunday afternoons, taught us
smoky Lapsang Souchong
high tea at the laden table,
Iolanthe on the old Victrola.

Then it was peppermint and sage,
licorice and hops, rose hips
and lemon balm. Skullcap
and passionflower,
the medicines for surviving
what the privatization of pain
calls stress.

Now *I* am the curandera,
listening, each morning and night
to what I want, body and soul.
Is it Ghost Pipe today,
the rare white angel of the northern woods?
Devil's Club like a hedge of thorns,
marshmallow and mullein for breath?

A day for milk thistle and dandelion
or licorice and red ginseng?

Ginger and turmeric staining the blender?
Lion's mane for the injured brain?
Blood orange and lemongrass
because I'm happy?
I move among my jars and bottles
crafting alliances with plants
far older than me, steeping help
from every cup, steeping prayer.

Six

BAÑOS

A bucket of rain water
fragrant leaves and flowers
I gather in the dusk
rose geranium, anise tarragon, mint,
wild ginger and pennyroyal
flowers of sauco, jasmine, rose.
I set the bucket out under the stars
under the moon.
At dawn I rise and heat the kettle
pour the steam into the brew
add juniper-scented gin
or dark cane rum
add honey.

I have no tub. I stand naked, shivering
in the cool mountain morning
and ladle the waters over my head,
let them trickle down, rub this essence
cross every inch of skin,
down to the soles of my feet.
Trouble runs off me like dust.
Trouble runs off me like dust.
Trouble runs off me
like dust.

Seven

HAMACA

We twist the threads of our days into string
knot it into nets, so the unneeded
falls through to the ground
and spines curved like nested birds,
we swing between two trees.
Hamaca, we said to el invasor
and soon we were filling their ships
with hammocks, a contagion of rest.
When I enter the half-moon embrace of cotton,
let go of steady and trade it for sway,
rock back and forth
with the rhythmic shifting of my mass,
like a child pumping a swing,
it dawns on me that this
is effortless davening,
immersed without ritual words
in my Arawak shabbat.

A Sweet Year of Struggle

A SWEET YEAR OF STRUGGLE

May we have a sweet year of struggle.
May we sing and hear our voices multiplied.
May we find the deep roots of courage in love
and feel it rise in us like sweet maple sap
simmered in the heat of this hard work,
the remaking of the world, until joy sugars our days.

Just as honey is made in the collective of shimmering wings
and sunshine grains of pollen gathered by many,
sin prisa, sin pausa, no hurry, no stopping,
let the joining of hands and hearts
seep from the many compartments of the comb
in a pool of liquid gold
and may the honey of our endeavors
drip, slow and delicious, onto our tongues.

May we have a sweet year of struggle.
May our losses fertilize the fields
into a bumper crop of blossom.
May the squashes flower and bear rich fruit.
May tomatoes and melons blush into flavor.
May all we have suffered turn
into soil. May a million mushrooms rise
from the broken places, and make medicine
for our wounding. May sunflowers clean the earth.

May we embrace the biggest challenges
we have ever faced, draw them close,
find their cracks and infiltrate like spores,
like tiny seeds, like moss.
May we turn our faces to the sun
and let hard times ripen in us,
until we are bursting with juice,
until we are blackberries among the thorns.
May we have a sweet year of struggle. Amen.

Ricardo Levins Morales

TASHLICH

I give the stones of my grief away,
let them slip like pebbles into the stream bed.
Into shallows where minnows flicker
I hurl them into the salty crash of wave on reef
as crabs scuttle into crevices.

My tiredness I surrender to the rain
to the tropical downpour, to the drawn out drizzle,
to the puddles after, to the percussion
of water drops on tin, pounding away at things,
to the shiny new leaves of the wild ginger
and the thirst-quenched ferns.

The ache of my body, the sickness, the scars
I lay out for the dew to spangle,
for condensation's slow caress to ease them
from my tight grip, away.

I must don high boots and heavy gear
to lay my jagged angers at the waterfall's foot
for the jackhammer of the torrent to unmake
and pound into gravel, into sand.

Empty handed I climb the bank
like ancient life emerging from the sea
dripping with possibility, evolving,
learning again, again, again,
to live on land.

SLICHAH FOR A SHMITA YEAR

let them go like birds released from cages
let them go like fruit rinds giving themselves to the soil
let them go like pebbles
rolling away underfoot on a steep trail
let them go like crumbs scattered for pigeons
let them go like sweat dripping from our brows

If we have messed up, let it go into the great compost heap
and become the nutrients for new seeds, intentions, blessings
pink blossomed, azure, ripe with tender food.
If others have hurt us, let clean water irrigate the wounds
and let the runoff water effortless gardens
that spring up between the furrows of sleeping fields
between the cracks of unswept sidewalks,
take over the untended lawns.

Let grudges crumble to dust.
Let shame dissolve into loam.
Let each harsh word we hurl at ourselves
be turned into petals scattering before they land.
Let everything, all of it, be recycled.
Let the trash become jewels we string into necklaces
and drape around each other's necks.

Let us enter the year of fallows
burdenless, loose-limbed,
lie down on the dark earth,
do nothing,
let tiny rootlets emerge from our fingers
let ourselves be covered with moss
and instead of doing
become the sapling students of the elder trees, and
be ourselves into the new year

and *be* ourselves toward the new world that waits
like an autumn bulb packed with unimagined colors
ready to wake and bloom
just under the skin of what is.

Lauryl Berger-Chun

Sukkot

These texts were created for a Sukkot celebration in Chicago, jointly sponsored by Tzedek Chicago and ChiNations Youth Council on reclaimed Indigenous land. Our sukkah was an unfinished wigwam. I rewrote two traditional texts, Psalm 137 and Numbers 24:5 (By the Rivers of Babylon and Ma Tovu) to fit not only the place and peoples present, but to include a broader range of exiles and comings together. My Lulav blessing names trees of the US Midwest, ties them to the four directions and elements, and calls on us to protect Earth, Fire, Air and Water.

EARTH SH'MA

Listen: There is no earth but this earth and we are its children. The earth is our home, and there is only one. The ground beneath our feet was millions of years in the making. Each leaf, each blade, each wing, each petal, each hair on the flank of a red fox, each scale on the sturgeon, each mallard feather, each pine needle and fragment of sassafras bark took millions of years to become, and we ourselves are millions of years in the making.

The earth offers itself and all its gifts freely, offers rain and sunlight, and the shimmer of moon on its lakes, offers corn and squash, apples and honey, salmon and lamb, and clear, cold water and all it asks in return is that we love it, respect its ways, cherish it.

So, we shall love the earth and all that lives with all our hearts, with all our souls, with all our intelligence, with all our might.

Oh wandering Jews, wherever we walk, wherever we sleep, wherever we eat, wherever we pray upon the face of the earth, we shall uphold the first peoples of that place, those who have loved it longest and know its ways most deeply.

We shall listen to them, learn from them, follow their lead, defend them, and join with them to protect each other and our world, and of every two grains in our bowls, we will give one to the first peoples who sit beside us at the earth's table.

The names of those who were here before us are syllables of the earth's name, so know them and speak them, and speak the first names for the places where you dwell, the water you drink, the winds that bring you breath. Say the name of this place, which is Shikaakwa, and say the names of its people: Anishinaabe, Odawa and Bodewadmi, the council of the three fires, the Asakiwaki and Meskwaki, people of the yellow earth and the red earth, the Ho-Chunk, the Myaamiaki and the Illiniwek, for the land held many stories before we came, many people lived here, and the places that were made for us were made by shattering their worlds.

Take to heart these words with which I charge you this day. Cherish this land beneath your feet. Cherish the roots and the waterways, the rocks and trees, the ancestor bones in the ground and the people who dance on the living earth and make new paths with their feet, with their breath, with their dreaming. Love and serve this world, this creation, as you love the creator who gifted it to us. Defend it from those whose hunger for riches cannot be filled, who devour and destroy, bringing death to everything we love.

Fight for the earth and protect it with all your heart and soul and strength, and hold nothing back, so that the rains fall in their season, the early rain and the late, and we may gather in the new grain, and wine, and oil, the squash, and beans, and corn, the apples, and grapes, and nuts, so that the grass grows high in the fields, and feeds the deer and the cattle, so that the water flows clean in river and lake, filled with abundant fish, and birds nest among the reeds, and all that lives shall eat its fill.

Do not be lured into the ways of consumption, for that which is consumed is the world. Do not be tempted to love comfort and convenience more than truth and right. Do not feast on oil, or use plastics as if they were as endless and easily unmade as autumn leaves. Do not partake in the desecration of the ancient dead whose bodies we burn as fuel. Do not bow down to the hoarders of what is good.

For if we do, the breath of life that is in all things will blow through the heavens and empty them of clouds. The rain will not fall and the earth will not yield its blessings, but will be laid waste, and there is no other earth.

So summon all the courage which is in you and in your people, stretching back to the dawn of time, make these words your own, and keep them close, by night and by day, with every breath you take, whatever you are doing. Let nothing stand in your way. Put your hands into the soil of this moment and plant good seed that we and all our children may live long in the land and be a blessing.

LULAV

Our blessings that are tied to specific lands are the easiest to rewrite for the truth of who and where we are today. Our lulav is woven of midwestern trees and the blessings of the four directions and elements.

EAST

This is Red Cedar, tree of dawn, whose smoke is a cleansing incense, whose scented boughs fill the forest with freshness. And this is the place of air.

We thank all the beings that exhale the air we inhale, the great rainforests, lungs of the world, the shimmering plankton, turning sunlight and seawater into oxygen. We thank for the wind that brings us rain, and dust and seed, and the migrating birds.

We give thanks for the voice of Creator in the wind, the breath of God on the waters, ruach chai, the breath of life.

We live in a time in which the sky itself is in danger, ripped apart by the gases of industry, the smoke of burning trees, the wakes of jet engines. When the heating atmosphere burns up the clouds and the sweet wind is choked with fumes. When heating oceans spawn immense, powerful storms that tear our worlds apart.

So we will become sky protectors, wind guardians, defenders of everything that makes air. We will interrupt the business as usual of pollution, and block the banks from their profits. We will befriend the wind and let it turn our mills and fill our sails. We will join with all the peoples of the earth, and stop the engines of extraction for the sake of breath.

SOUTH

This is persimmon, pechamin, flame colored fruit of autumn, shaped like the human heart, holding the place of fire.

We give thanks for the fire of the sun that gives life to all things.
We give thanks for the sacred fires of memory that hold our stories.
We give thanks for the gift of fire that cooks our food, warms our bodies,
keeps us safe, and makes a gathering place. We give thanks for the double
candle flame that gathers us to prayer, and the fire of our own hearts.

We say in the words of poet Adrienne Rich that we are:

> with the rowboat ice-fast on the shore
> in the last red light of the year
> that knows what it is, that knows it's neither
> ice nor mud nor winter light
> but wood, with a gift for burning.

We live in a time when fire rages uncontrolled across the world, ignited
by greed: cattle ranchers and palm oil planters setting fire to the Amazon.
Wildfires sparked by unmaintained cables choking California, Oregon and
Washington in smoke. Fires searing through the rainforests of West Africa
and the Siberian Taiga. When colonizers try to desecrate the sacred volcano
of Mauna Kea, looking at the distant fire of stars instead of the sacred fires
around them on the earth.

We who are fire keepers will tend the living flame of our people and pass it
from hand to hand. We children of the burning bush that is never consumed
will keep the fire of spirit alive in us. We will let the sun heat our houses and
light our nights. We will use energy wisely, tend the land with fire, make
ash to feed the soil and clear away tinder. We will interrupt the burning of
our ancient ancestors to fuel the endless hunger for more. We will feed the
sparks of courage within and between us, and join with all the people of the
world, in a blaze of hope and purpose, restore our creative fire and ignite a
global culture of reciprocity and generosity as the beating heart of human
life on earth.

WEST

This is Willow, tree of the water's edge, whose leaves flow like streams, whose wands are the bones of basketry and longhouses, and this is the place of water. Here by the vast lakes that hold one of every five drops of fresh water in the world.

We give thanks for the rain that falls to earth and fills the rivers and lakes, that makes the corn rise, the fruit swell, the tight bud open into bloom. We give thanks for the quenching of thirst, for washing our bodies clean, for the rivers that move through our flesh. We give thanks for great blue glaciers and tropical downpours, for thundering cascades and delicate dew. We praise the living being we call water, that flows in and out of red veins and green, making a tracery of drops spangling the globe, this wet planet of our birth, this single organism we are. We are made of water's dance.

There is no good English for Mni Wichoni because English has turned a living being always in motion into an object, a noun, but in Hebrew we say mayyim chayim, the living waters.

And yet everywhere water is in danger. Huge dams choke the flow of rivers to make more power for the powerful. Industrial poisons seep into aquifers, gush into the Gulf, spill out of pipelines, spread across pools in the Ecuadorian Amazon, corrode the pipes that now carry brown sludge to the faucets of Flint. As the world heats, green places go dry, and oceans rise up to drown island nations. Rivers overflow their banks and sweep our homes away. Storm surges wash us into the sea.

Guakía guakiáchi ni. We will love and protect the waters. We will lift up the charter of the Great Lakes Commons, stop pipelines and hydroelectric dams, reforest the naked slopes where roots hold water and branches draw down rain. We will get in the way of pillage with these bodies filled with rain. We will join with all the people of the earth to make a new deal that is both green and red, and we will pray for the rain to keep falling.

Send to us the angel Af-Bri, trailing showers of rain to soften the face of the wasteland when it is dry as rock. Soothe our spirits and bring us back to life. You who make the wind blow and the rain descend, who kindled the sun and moon and stars, and formed the earth on which we live, grant us water as a blessing and not a curse, for life and not for death, for abundance without thirst, amen.

NORTH

This is maple, shaped like our hands, sweetness in its veins, just beneath the skin, ablaze with colors as varied as the earth itself, and this is the place of earth, soil, rock, clay.

We give thanks to water, fire and ice for grinding rock into dirt. We give thanks to all the creatures who dying, made soil, and to the soil, full of life, erupting into leaf and blade. We give thanks to the ancestors who made the black earth of the Amazon by burying compost and charcoal for thousands of years. We give thanks to our mother who feeds us from her body.

We say the earth is not real estate. The earth is alive. We say the earth has no borders or property lines. The earth is alive.

The Earth holds our ancient dead, and deep under our feet, the graves of our ancestors' ancestors, ancient phytoplankton pressed and simmered over aeons into paleo-blackstrap, fossilized sunlight, the thing we call petroleum.

We will not allow the desecration of the dead in the name of money. We will turn our world toward the sun and wind. We will not allow this earth to become a burnt offering to the gods of wealth.

We say the earth is hurting. Eroded hills, dust on the wind, drought turning the fertile ground to cracked and barren wastes. Soil washing into sea, land disappearing from the gulf coast lands of the Houma a football field an hour. Islands around the world swallowed up by rising seas and melting ice caps. Soil weakened and leached of nourishment, so it no longer grows crops, and farmers must walk a thousand miles to a border lined with cages trying to find food.

We say we will feed the farmers and the soil, open the cages, push back the bulldozers and replant the slopes. We say the earth is the mother of all of us, and no one has the right to possess her. We say we will heal the earth and defend her. We say we will sink our roots into the ground and we shall not be moved. We say the earth is not for sale.

With Nicolás Guillén we say:

> Can you sell me the earth, the deep night
> of roots, dinosaur teeth and the scattered lime
> of distant skeletons?
> Can you sell me long buried jungles, dead birds,
> fishes of stone, volcanic sulfur, a thousand
> million years rising in a spiral? Puedes
> Venderme tierra, can you
> sell me land, can you?
>
> The earth that is yours is mine.
> All of our feet walk it.
> Nobody owns it, no one.

East, South, West and North the beautiful world unfolds around us, with all its gifts and dangers. There are struggles to join, people to join with, and works to do in every direction. So let us feast together, nourish our bodies and our spirits and grow strong.

RIVERS/TENTS

All of us here have lost connections to ancestral lands, some many thousands of years ago, some in the last few centuries, some just the other day. All of us have losses to grieve. Jews are settlers in this land. Our ancestors came from other continents, many of us fleeing danger, hoping for freedom, and many of us never looked back. But in order to be fully present with you, here and now and in the days to come, we need to grieve those losses. In order to be connected with this earth right here, we must weep for the lands we lost.

By all the rivers of our many exiles, we have sat down and wept, as we remembered the lands of our ancestors, the lands that were stolen from us, the places we were stolen and driven from.

We wept as we remembered birdsong in the meadows of Andalusía and moonrise over Baghdad, the cold winds of autumn off the steppes and argan trees in the valley of the River Draa, ripening pomegranates of Jerusalem, apple orchards blossoming in Ukraine.

We wept as we remembered the waterfalls of Yukiyú, the scent of guavas and seawater, towering trunks of ausubo, guayacán, capá. We wept as we remembered the wild rice beds of the north, the singing of loons, all the forests and river banks of the Anishinaabe, the windswept beauty of Lakota grasslands, ribbons of light over ancient homelands in the deep north, the long ago eastern woodlands of maple and beech, left behind as our peoples were pushed westward by settlers from across the sea. We wept, remembering the volcanoes and lakes of the K'iché and Kaqchikel, the rivers and islands of Lenca and Miskito, the desert springs of the Nahua.

We wept, remembering rainforests and savannas, the red rice marshes of Mali and the tulip trees of Ghana, the lapping of waves in the mangroves where the Niger meets the sea.

We sat on the ground and wept our grief, and we hung our flutes and drums and the songs of our hearts upon the willows, for those who carried us away into captivity, those who drove us at sword point and gunpoint from the lands that our people knew and loved, those who stole our children and silenced our languages, those who laid waste to the earth, demanded of us that we sing and dance for them, that we entertain them, that we wear costumes, that we work the comedy circuit telling jokes that ridiculed our families, that we turn the stories of our peoples into gift-shop souvenirs and mascots for their sports teams, that we get over it, that we assimilate or die, that we be cheerful.

But how can we sing creators' songs when our roots have been torn from the ground that made us, our languages smothered, our children taken away to be raised by our captors in a world of punishment? We begin without words, to sing our grief together.

We are windblown seeds, uprooted a thousand times and blown across oceans to this place. We are from seven days walk north along the lake shore, pushed here by glaciers of greed. We are from the islands south and east of here, brought on wings of storm, and if we all carry grief in the palm of one hand, in the other we hold tight to joy, for we are still here, breathing the air, alive in spite of everything, fulfilling our ancestors' dreams.

No matter how many times we've had to leave our homes, no matter how many burning villages are at our backs, we carry creator's song within us, everywhere we go, praising the beauty of this flowering earth and all its peoples, and rooting ourselves in kinship with each other and all living things. This is the shelter we weave with our hands working together. Our friendships are our beautiful tents, and for this hour, we have pitched them here.

Ma tovu: How beautiful and good are the tents of our peoples.

Ma tovu ohalecha Anishinaabe, mishkenotecha Yisrael.
Ma tovu ohalayech Potawatomi, mishkenotechem Mizrahim.
Ma tovu ohalechem Romaniotim, mishkenotecha Ho-Chunk.
Ma tovu ohalayech Arawaka, mishkenotechen yoshvot teyvel.

FENCE POSTS

I am a Caribbean Jew. My father's family farmed and made clothing in southern Ukraine. My mother's people farmed and made clothing in Puerto Rico, Connecticut and New York. They have roots seven thousand years old in Boriken, now known as Puerto Rico, and in northern Iberia, North and West Africa.

I am both Indigenous and settler, colonizer and colonized. It has taken many, many tellings of my tangled family stories to people who listened deeply, many tears and shivers, much shouting and laughter to find my ease in all the difficulty of that knot.

I came to understand that Russia's imperial dreams, and its antisemitism, repeatedly forced my Jewish ancestors to uproot and settle on other people's land. We were expendable so we were sent to hold down borders.

In 1808, the Tsars set my family to farming the southern Ukrainian lands of native Tatars, making us a living barrier against the Ottoman Turks. In 1904, Russia and Japan went to war over Manchuria and my great grandfather fled the draft to Lenape land in New York. In the 1930s his little sister and her family were persuaded to settle in Birobidzhan, on tribal lands along the easternmost border with China. We were planted like fence posts.

In 1951, my blacklisted New York City parents came to this ancestral Arawak land where I now live. My mother brought her Boricua feminist rebellion back to the homeland, and my father brought the best of his Jewish radicalism, once rooted in Ukrainian soil, to the red clay of Indiera.

How does a fence post root and bloom? Turn back into a tree?

Stop securing the borders of colonial occupations? Open them instead?

Telling and feeling these contradictory stories, being listened to as I explored what they meant to me, brought me closer to my Jewish

ancestors, to understanding their complexity, their difficult choices, and to
write this poem, on my Indigenous people's land, about how to carry a settler
legacy with integrity.

LAND DAYS

Every day is a land day somewhere.
People land upon each other,
steal the way the light fell through
particular trees that are gone,
tear up villages and gardens
as if they were weeds, weed out
particular people who are gone
from land that no longer holds
the way their laughter drifted through
open doors along with the smells
of their cooking. We land and are
landed upon, so what

does the windblown milkweed
seed say to the field's edge, already filled
with fireflies and sassafras,
what does the tulipán say
shouldering in among roble blanco,
capá prieto? We choose, we

settlers in the grass, we
un-native to these fields,
these felled woods, these
cane fields and cafetales,
these houses built over graves,
we get to decide, we do not
have to be invasive

maybe the milkweed
rests lightly among the cattails
listening to the night

listening to how each part
sings, how the birches

and the earthworms
are speaking, we could
be like that, we could

listen, all our lives

be like the common
plantain, low to the
ground, rooting only
where there is room
between the conversations
of moss and stars,

join, not destroy, the ecosystems
join, not erase, the whole story

listen to the particular
crimes committed.
lean into their cold truth,
say yes this happened.
taste the ash of it, without
turning away, without lying about
any of it, yes we could

shred the deeds to
these houses built over graves
these manicured, gated
fictions about who
has the right to what, and tell

on ourselves, tell how our
family photographs, people
with our noses, eyes, hair
fleeing hunger, war, pogroms,
therefore always

one foot out the door,
tried to buy belonging, force
other people's land to be home.

we could stay, both feet here
we could change
ourselves, not the stolen land.
become something else.

not, no matter how long we stay,
not native, we could just
root where we are,
in the crux of history
in the truth of it all

not so the land will belong to us

it can never
it is full of other people's stories
we do not need to own their losses
or the way the light fell,
we do not need to
rename everything after
ourselves, piña is not an apple,
we lost the apples
we came across water in
leaky boats, we miss
a different light

but so that we can

not clearcut history, not plow
the wildflowers of the prairie
into acreage, but lie down in it
and be stained, overgrown,

we could adapt, cross-pollinate, become
naturalized, become common,
he low to the ground, rest lightly
honor the people, still here,
long before us

belong to the land.

Wendy Somerson

Pesach

In the early 1980s in the San Francisco Bay Area, I began taking part in and writing for liberation seders that linked ancient ritual with contemporary liberation movements and moments. During the writing of this book, I worked with two groups to create new texts for their haggadot. In Detroit, I worked with Tchiyah synagogue and Detroit Jews for Justice to create new blessings for the four cups of seder wine. In New Orleans I worked extensively with the local chapter of Jewish Voice for Peace to create language that spoke to the universal longing for safety. In this section I include excerpts from both those projects, as well as individual pieces written over many years of being a haggadist.

FOOD AS RITUAL: A BRIEF MEMOIR

Inca potatoes are made into Indian curry, German potato salad, Irish leek soup, and Ashkenazi latkes. Chinese oranges grown in Spanish groves become English marmalade. California farms grow kiwi from northern China, Persian melons, and Mesoamerican beans. The sweet potatoes of tropical South America become a staple in China, Korea and Japan. Whether we're fleeing war and natural disaster, seeking trade and new resources, or fall captive, enslaved for the enrichment of others, people have been moving for as long as we've been people, and our foods move with us.

The knowledge of our home cuisines goes with us into exile, into captivity, into migration. We carry tiny pockets of precious seeds sewn into our clothing or hidden in our hair, find substitutes for long-lost condiments, vegetables and meats, and wherever we are, we experiment, exchange and combine flavors with neighbors, pair Asian rice with American beans, add American tomatoes to Italian focaccia, and invent California rolls in L.A.

I grew up in the mountains of Western Puerto Rico with two New York–born parents, one Puerto Rican Catholic and one Ashkenazi Jew with roots in Ukraine, who blended two cuisines that were already the result of thousands of years of migrations, invasions, captivity, and commerce.

My maternal Puerto Rican cuisine is the result of Arab trade routes, the Spanish invasion of the Americas, and the Atlantic slave trade. It is built on rice, citrus and chicken carried from Southeast Asia to Spain by Arab merchants; Mediterranean olive oil, olives, raisins and oregano; Mesoamerican beans, avocados, tomatoes, peppers and corn; Indigenous Caribbean seafood, bananas, greens, and roots (yautía, yuca, malanga, boniato, ñame), West African herbs, spices, vegetables, and transplanted Southeast Asian plantains, and above all, the adaptive genius to blend African recipes and techniques with Caribbean ingredients.

My paternal cuisine grew from the farms and shtetls of Eastern Europe, the beets and buckwheat, eggs and dairy, onions and apples of Eurasia, potatoes brought from the Andes, Mediterranean eggplants, chickens from Southeast Asia, cinnamon from India, white fish and pickles, cabbages, and the wheat I can no longer eat.

My mother grew up in Harlem and later the Bronx, surrounded by migrants. Picked on by the Italian and Irish kids, she made alliances with Eastern European Jews, and grew up eating blintzes and kosher dills in the homes of her friends. For my father, eggs, dairy, tomatoes, and sugar were the four food groups. So, he Ashkenazified guacamole by removing jalapeños and adding hard boiled eggs. It was after he met my mother that he became the world's best Jewish tostón maker.

My parents moved to Puerto Rico in 1951 because they were blacklisted communists facing my father's possible drafting into the Korean war. They bought an abandoned coffee farm and raised vegetables and hens, selling produce and eggs from the back of a battered pickup truck, and astonished the neighbors by eating sautéed greens, snow peas and chard, cottage cheese and egg salad with our rice and beans and fried plantain.

In that remote mountain community, we were the only Jews we knew, but Jews have been in the Caribbean since the very earliest days of the European invasion. Sephardic Jews, expelled from Portugal and Spain, joined Europe's imperialist venture as slave traders and merchants. They settled on Indigenous land, and participated in the same crimes of genocide and slavery as their Christian counterparts. They also took part in social justice movements against colonialism, for abolition, and feminism, and the rights of workers. By the 18th century, half the Jewish population of the Americas lived in the Caribbean and the mainland Dutch colony of Suriname. There were many Jews hidden among the early Spanish settlers of the Antilles, but if they were among my ancestors, the evidence has been lost.

My paternal family left Ukraine between 1890 and 1906. My great-grandfather Abraham went to Canada and then New York. His first cousin Alter went to Argentina, where many of his descendants still live, though one branch also ended up in Puerto Rico. For two Jews from the little Ukrainian village of Yazer, Brooklyn and Buenos Aires were equally strange, but to my US Ashkenazi relatives who have fully assimilated into whiteness, to most white US Jews, Caribbean and Latin American Jews seem an improbable, exotic oddity. And when my Brooklyn father and Harlem mother joined forces and produced three children who are also Caribbean Indigenous, West and North African and Iberian, our existence itself became incomprehensible, incredible, at best a quirky sidebar to the dominant narrative of US Jewish identity, at worst, an impossibility that white people, Jewish and not, literally can't wrap their minds around.

As a young adult in the Bay Area in the early 1980s, I was part of an up-surge of Jewish lesbian feminist and other radical revisions to traditional Jewish celebrations. I was working at La Peña Cultural Center, founded by Chilean exiles after the 1973 military coup, and wrote a hagaddah that interwove the stories of Central American political refugees with the Exodus. But this cultural movement, like all the Jewish communities I had come across, was dominated by white Ashkenazi Jews to whom my Puerto Rican identity made no sense, and was either tokenized or ignored.

One way I began to assert myself in those spaces was by inventing Puerto Rican twists on Ashkenazi recipes. In the food memoir I'm writing I reveal the plantain as a quintessential Caribbean Jewish food (and a great gluten-free substitute for matzo and matzo balls), share Picaflor, the appetizer that Cuban Jewish anthropologist Ruth Behar and I invented, that pairs lox, white cheese, and guava paste, and celebrate Mango Charoset, which I dreamed up after some-one told me about the 18th century, sand-floored synagogue in St. Thomas, the oldest continuously operating synagogue in US territory, and I started imagining an ancient Caribbean seder of our own. And because I am a child of storytellers, because I learned to cook on the wood fires of illiterate elders and measure ingredients by their weight in my hands, my recipes are not formulae. They're legends.

MANGO CHAROSET

You begin with ripe mangoes, firm enough not to disintegrate when diced, but already almost unbearably sweet. Sniff each skin, press each fruit for just the right amount of give. Pick enough to fill your arms, and go home. With a sharp knife, cut parallel to the pit, all the way through, making two flushed cheeks, dripping with juice. Cross-hatch the inner flesh, cutting all the way to the peel. Then flip it inside out, so the cubes of mango pop up like an old-fashioned swimming cap. Tickle the pieces away, and drop them into a big bowl. (After that, you attack the pit with your teeth, and tear away the fibers until there is nothing but a bone-white, chewed-up seed and juice all over your face.)

Fruit, nuts, alcohol and spice are the essentials of charoset. But don't imagine apples, walnuts and wine. Start chopping handfuls of candied ginger and dropping them into the bowl. Peel a couple of ripe limes, dice the rind, and squeeze the juice into the mixture. Your hands will be sticky. Go ahead and lick them. Now stir in a whole lot of grated coconut, fresh if you can, or at least moist. Sometimes I add chopped pecans, tipping my hat toward the Algonquians of North America, in the sweet sunny south before plantations. Now come the spices: Antillean allspice and cayenne from what is now Guyana, Moluccan nutmeg, white pepper of India, and pan-South Asian cardamom. Mix it with your hands, kneading it together, inhaling the mingling of acid and sweet, hot and delicate.

The last touch is the rum. The spirits. The touch of fire. Choose a good dark one. How much do you like the people you're cooking for? If you love them very much, use all your pull to hustle up some Barrilito, the very best Puerto Rican rum there is, made by a nationalist who refuses to mass market to the US. Three-star is hard to get outside the island, but with luck, you can get two-star. If you live far from a barrio, it's fine to go with another brand. The Bacardi family fled revolution from Cuba to Puerto Rico, leaving behind a B-shaped swimming pool at their former estate in Havana, where I got rehab after my stroke. I use their rum to toast their involuntary contribution to socialist medicine. Any rum you choose is loaded with history. Sugar and rum stoked the engines of genocide, slavery and war in the Caribbean for centuries, but rum was invented by slaves who experimented with fermenting molasses, seeking solace, celebration, and survival. Caribbean charoset pays tribute to our own resistance and survival, our conspiracies and uprisings, subversion and persistence, and acknowledges the deep suffering that has also shaped us. So, make it early in the day, and give the rum and ginger, spices and juices time to mingle and saturate each other, and become something sweet and strong and hot, enough to go on with.

THE EVOLVING SEDER PLATE

Please feel free to add verses

Here's where we riff on the fight of the moment,
here's where we shoot for the moon,
here's where the possible's on the table
and everyone's in the room.

Oranges, olives, beetroot and spoons.

Glowing orange segments
bless every kind of love
and every shade of gender
fills the world we're dreaming of.

Oranges, olives, beetroot and spoons.

The olive is for Palestine
our dear beloved kin
how the peace that comes from justice
is how everybody wins.

Oranges, olives, beetroot and spoons.

The blood-red beet represents all those
who lost the right to own our wombs
who bear the babes we cannot raise
or bleed out in back alley rooms.

Oranges, olives, beetroot and spoons.

Persimmons, roasted corn, pecans,
cranberries red and wild rice black
tell us the only thing to do
with stolen land is give it back.

Oranges, olives, beetroot and spoons.

FOUR CUPS

CUP ONE: A THOUSAND THREADS

We raise this cup to the garment of a thousand threads, the coat of twenty million colors, for the heart of the Jewish world lives equally in every Jew, and no one is exotic, and every one of us is Jewish enough, and however we travel through the world is a Jewish path.

To the Baghdadi Jews of India, and the Afroashkenazim of Harlem and Capetown. To late-night klezmer jazz, to leaflets and marches, and kosher soul food. To the Sephardim of Recife in Brazil, the Maghrebi Jews of Fez in Morocco, and the Palestinian Jews of Jerusalem. To the Chinese Jews of Kaifeng and San Francisco. To the Abayudaya of Uganda, the Beta Israel of Ethiopia, the Bene Israel of India. To the Bukharan Jews of Tashkent and the Romaniote of Corfu and Corinth. To a new definition of Jewish food.

To the Jewyorican born of Manhattan garment sweatshops, public schools, and strikes. To Rosa Collazo and Ethel Rosenberg knitting together in the common room of their prison, to my aunt Eva Levins the radical hat maker, living next door to Jesus Colón the radical journalist. To Manilatown Jews of Seattle and Albuquerque Crypto-Chicanim, to Choctaw Jews of Biloxi and the tango-dancers of Moisesville in Argentina.

To Jews who enter the tent from every point of the compass, through the waters of birth and the waters of the mikvah. Let there be taco-brie. Let there be saffron with cinnamon, Yemeni hot sauce and pickled lemons, latkes made of yuca, sweet potato kugel, mango charoset, Chinese Five Spice Challah and Kobe brisket, rose water chicken and crysanthemum tea.

To never again saying Jew when we mean white Jew. To never again saying Jewish culture when we mean Yiddishkeit. To never again applying the crooked mathematics of blood quantum to any human being. There is no such thing as half a Jew.

To the day when we sit in the center of every Jewish space, and don't explain ourselves, and nobody is confused. To the day when wherever we sit becomes the heart of the Jewish world.

CUP TWO: TO CLARITY

A cup of clarity, a cup to reveal the workings of a vast machine whose engine is greed, and all the different wheels that engine turns. A cup to show how the teeth of the wheels interlock.

Imagine racism is a millstone, a crushing weight that grinds and presses down relentlessly on people intended to be a permanent underclass. Its purpose is to extract the oil of profit from us, right to the edge of extermination and beyond. It presses and crushes and grinds, but the people push back and it generates heat that begins to rise. If the owners of the mill, their hands on the switches and cranks, don't insulate themselves, it will all get too hot to handle.

Imagine the oppression of Jews is that insulation, a pressure valve, a shunt that redirects the steaming rage of working people away from the mostly white and Christian 1%, who own the machine and collect the oil pressed from our lives. Imagine a valve they can open at will, a pipe that diverts the scalding heat off to the side. For Jews to be blamed for oppression, some of us must be seen to prosper, must be well paid and highly visible, positioned as the public faces of an inequality we help to administer, but do not own. The purpose of oppressing Jews is not to crush us day after day. It's to have us available for crushing. To be the bone they throw.

Nobody sees the owners. They don't let their faces appear on the cover of *Time* and *Newsweek*. They hire us to be their faces. They send us to collect taxes. They appoint us as judges. Long before they let us live in their neighborhoods, they let us manage their inner city buildings full of brown people. And some of us agree. And some of us don't. But they keep telling stories about how we're greedy. When they cut 500 million dollars from the budget of the City University of New York, they tell the working class people of color who study there that the reason isn't that they hate public universities. The reason, they say, is that the people of color have upset the Jews. We are 1.7% of the world's people and 1.7% of the world's rich, but they say we are the reason people are poor.

Imagine the people under the grindstone are in a fury, marching down the road toward where the owners live. Imagine the oppression of Jews is a conjuring trick that works through misdirection, that the Protestant heirs of slaveholder fortunes, pilgrim entrepreneurs and railroad barons grown rich from stealing Indigenous land, the people who gamble with our mortgages, shoot our children, poison our water and break the circle of seasons are holding a great big DETOUR sign with red arrows pointing toward the Jews, and some of the marchers on the road begin to think the problem with Jewish financiers is that they are Jewish, not that they are financiers, that the problem with Jewish slumlords is that they are Jewish, not that they are slumlords. They don't notice that nobody ever says Presbyterian banker, Baptist slumlord. Some of them wander onto the side road, the momentum of their fury drains away into resentment, and they talk about Jews instead of class, begin to think maybe Jews ARE class. The steam thins out and blows away and the owners are safe for another day.

So, here's a cup to the end of deception. Here's a cup to watching their hands. Here's a cup to steam under pressure, to no more grindstones and no more valves. May we all be the wrench in the gears.

CUP THREE: TO SANCTUARY

We raise this cup to sanctuary, to the places that become holy because we shelter each other there. We raise this cup to escape. To the doors we open through fences and walls. To the rivers we ferry each other across. To the journey from danger to refuge.

Everywhere rulers find someone to blame. They use the language of contamination, infection, infestation, epidemic, speak of cleansing their countries, pass laws, send soldiers, build holding pens, and people are blown across the map like dust. Everywhere people risk themselves in makeshift rafts, creep under wire, hide in cellars and gullies, find passage, pay bribes, beg shelter.

526 years ago tomorrow, the monarchs of a newly formed Spain issued their edict of expulsion and drove at least 40,000 Iberian Jews into exile, and they went, carrying the keys to their stolen houses, occupied by strangers, handing them down across generations.

Three days from today, lawyers will debate in Israeli courts the plan to drive 40,000 African asylum seekers into the arms of waiting slavers and executioners. If they are stripped of everything, to whom will they give their keys?

70 years ago this May, 750,000 Palestinians were driven from their land and their towns demolished to lay the foundations of settler houses. Their keys were scattered to the four quarters of exile, but like compass needles they keep pointing the way home. Yesterday thirty thousand gathered at the edge of that exile and soldiers on duty during the feast of freedom killed seventeen people simply for being where they were.

One month ago on Sunday, our sister Siwatu and her unborn child were sentenced to prison because she tried to defend herself and her family from violent assault, and the laws that protect white men with guns did not protect her. Can we become the key that will open her cell? Lift a cup to the makers of refuge, to the lantern in a window, to the secret attic, to the loaf in the haystack and the water jug in the desert. To the falsified papers, to the loan of a name, to the pro bono lawyer, to the crowds at the airports.

Lift a cup to the ending of borders. To the end of all danger. To the end of all harm. To the day when we migrate like sea turtles and swallows, like pollen and dust, like songs and ideas, to free passage everywhere under the sun. And here's to the day when no one is uprooted, to digging in deeper in the places where we are, to universal safety and the right to remain. Lift a cup to the sanctuary planet we dream.

CUP FOUR: TO DREAMING

We raise this cup to that world that rises like steam from our dreaming. To lifting our eyes for a moment from the difficult road.

May we dwell in the place where joy meets justice,
so in love with a vision of what's possible that we no longer flirt with despair.

The world is full of weather, full of all the urgency
and danger of the present moment,
but the work of justice has always been urgent.
Here is a cup for the time and space to dream together, dream big,
and set a real course toward our dreaming.

The moment will come, I swear it,
when we will trust enough in who we are and will become,

when the past will weigh less than the possible,
in which our scars will transform themselves
into tattoos of our histories. In one hand,
we will carry individual autonomy,
and in the other the broadest and deepest solidarity,
and they will beat their perfect rhythm on the drums of daily life.

It won't be on a holiday, with speeches and parades.
It won't be in the ceremony of signing treaties
and taking oaths of office, nor at the moment
when the last flag of empire
ceases to cast its shadow on any ground.
It will be an ordinary Tuesday,
in the middle of washing dishes perhaps,
but between one heartbeat and the next,
we will realize that on that day, we woke up free.

Arielle Tonkin

FOUR ANCESTORS

THE ANCESTOR WHO HIDES

I am the one who bides my time, who hid my face, who changed my name, who put the mezuzah inside the madonna, the orisha in the saint, the archives of the ghetto in a milk can underground. I passed on the knowledge of our history in secret, only lit candles behind shuttered windows, camouflaged my meaning in a layered song, whispered forbidden languages at night, and I saved myself and others through deceit. I lived in a closet, in a cellar, went underground, wore a disguise, changed my accent, my clothes, my food, the way I walked, became someone else each time I left my house. For centuries this is how I survived, keeping only the smallest flame of us alive. I watched and listened, kept a record, carried messages, was a model prisoner, always lowered my eyes, and worked in secret for the common good. I know how to speak in code, to recognize the others, to make a sign, to infiltrate, to pass as someone else, to save what matters most and leave the rest behind. I choose to live and fight another day, live til I have a chance to get away, carry the seeds of other times within, and wear my secret like another skin. I am alive, but after so long in hiding, who do I know, and who in the world knows me? When it's time to open the doors and windows wide, what if I can't find the key? My strength is to reckon up the odds, avoid the battles that I know I'll lose, and even though I count the heavy cost, because we live, not everything is lost.

THE ANCESTOR WHO RUNS

I am the ancestor who runs, who carries the magic of escape, who knows the borders of captivity, each link of chain, each post. Who stows away, slips under barbed wire, swims the river, disappears into untilled land. I jump the train, head for the hills, go into the swamps, follow the drinking gourd, forge the papers, bribe a guard, dig a tunnel, pay a smuggler, go into exile, carry my life in my pocket, eat where I can. My map is a song, a quilt, a riddle, a name someone said to memorize and not write down. Somebody told me there's a safer place than here, so I navigate by possibility and fear. My strength is to risk my life for something better, to take a chance and leave the devil I know, to break the line, to run for the woods, to cut the rope, no more *heigh ho heigh ho and off to work I go.* But when I run, who do I leave behind? Who else's lives do I risk? And when I arrive, whose homes lie underfoot, what if my coming makes new refugees? Or do I keep running, never taking root, my promised land just over the horizon, round the bend? I ask you to think outside the box, beyond the borders of your lives. To leave the familiar and take a chance on something new. What if the dream that seems impossible is true?

THE ANCESTOR WHO BUILDS

I am the ancestor who takes root right where I am. I plant food in empty lots, and organize to stop the local dam, the prison over the hill, the incinerator upwind, the neighborhood gentrification plan. Day after day I plant and hoe and weed, fighting to build just a piece of what we need. Each time we win an inch, somebody lives, somebody gets the strength to take the next step and the next. The decent housing we can afford can shelter the dream of something more. I open freedom schools in storefronts, take over city councils, sink a well, start language classes so children will know their elders, make worker co-ops in the factories and fields, send books and water filters, tents and solar lights. I am a cup of water in a dry land. I am a lantern in the night. I build a little piece of freedom, but is it just for those whose names I know? I rig a shelter from the storm, but am I settling for staying dry, while wind and water rage and others drown? Did I make a country out of other people's pain, learn to accept that their loss was my gain? Working night and day for what seems practical but small, will I forget to plant the seeds of a bigger liberation for us all? Did I cut down the leaves and stems of injustice and leave the root intact? My strength is making hope concrete, making it real, inspiration we can see and touch and feel. The lesson of my junkyard garden plot of food and flowers: each time you win an inch, reach for a mile. Hope builds on hope, and acting powerful builds power. But never settle for a little patch of sun. Push back the shadows til it shines on everyone.

THE ANCESTOR WHO CONFRONTS

I am *arise you prisoners of starvation*, I am the walkout, the strike, the plantation house in flames, the raid on the settler town, the wheelchairs chained to fences, the ones who link arms and won't be moved, the ones who sit down, occupy, block roads, say no. I am the uprising, the overthrow, the revolution in the streets and in the hills. I go face to face, hand to hand, toe to toe. I shout from the rooftops, I hold the line, I make demands. Right here, right now is where I make my stand. Safety will only come when we have won, torn down the palaces, and broken all the guns. If we win, there will be nothing to run away from. If we lose, there will be nowhere on earth to run. My strength is to push back, to break down walls and break the tyrant's rule, to mobilize and fill the streets, to sue them for our future, to beat the drums, to make their everyday impossible, to disrupt, to tell the truth they want to hide, to bring the consequences home. But sometimes I hurl myself right at the wall and break my bones. Sometimes I burn out like a torch. Sometimes I'm hoarse from shouting, and can no longer sing. Sometimes I forget that fighting isn't everything.

SONG OF THE NARROW PLACE

to the tune of "Brother Can You Spare a Dime?"

Once I built a warehouse, to store the grain
and keep the hungry in line.
Once I built a warehouse, all locked and chained
but none of the grain was mine.
Once I built a pyramid up to the sun
of brick and mortar and lime,
that cast its shadow on everyone
for a very long, long time.

When Pharaohs send their armies in
they seize the land,
they take our children away.
We're deep in struggles, can't seem to win
working double for half the pay.

Sometimes at night I dream that we all have enough
of food and shelter and ease,
though times are hard and the living is rough,
sometimes I dream we're free.

THE EDGE

This is the place where the way is blocked, the end of the road, the edge
of the land where we've been making do, making it through, just getting
by from day to day. Here's where we decide: do we lie down, give up, ask
nothing more than to deaden pain, or is this where patience runs out and
resignation goes up in flames?

This tumultuous sea is where we choose to act, step off the land, right into
the tide, sick and tired of being sick and tired, determined now to reach the
other side.

This is when we threw down our tools and walked off the job, walked out of
school, voted to strike, sat down in the road, when we spoke the forbidden
language at the top of our lungs. This is the moment of enough is enough.

When one child too many was gunned down for breathing.
When crowds marched to the border, demanding return.
When the landlord raised the rent again, and we wouldn't pay.
When the union bosses said accommodate,
but young Clara Lemlich climbed up on a table
yelling strike now, because we will not wait.
When we walked to work in Montgomery.
When we took our boats to Alcatraz.
When we said not in my name, no more.
When we marched against the Viet Nam War.
When children walked out of classrooms in Soweto, in Managua,
last month in their millions all around the world.
When we lost our patience. When our outrage was bigger than our fear.
When we said boycott, sanction, divest. When we said Sí Se Puede.
When we said water is life, we will defend it. When we said
Black. Lives. Matter.

At first we'll walk through the muck, hands clasped in a long chain of
travelers, leaving the old life behind, everything we learned to live with, put
up with, dying of it day by day, the mud of it dragging at our shoes. But as

we walk into the water and keep walking deeper and deeper, even though the waves slap at our faces, we'll know this is how it happens. This is how the sea parts, the road opens, this is how things change.

So what is the edge you're standing at? Are you ready to wade into this water now and part this sea? What do you leave behind you, what are ready to push through, what will you not take anymore, what is your destination on the other shore?

WANDERING

When we came to the desert, after all the singing and dancing, we looked around and saw a dry land to the edge of the sky and no roads. We were tired, our feet were blistered, and we carried generations of trauma in our muscles and our bones. We sat in the sand and tried to draw a map of our safety, but the wind blew it away.

We knew we were not alone there but we didn't believe it. Other groups of people passed in the distance, looking for who knows what. It wasn't our business. We had our own problems to solve. We watched them warily. We didn't ask.

We said first things first, pitch the tents, build fires, draw water from Miriam's wandering well. This is the circle of what we can afford to care about. After all, the manna won't last forever, and we were chosen to receive it. We avoided those other tents, the glow of their fires in the dusk. The freedom we were promised was for us, the tribe, the nation, our relatives, the ones whose names we could pronounce. Choosing each other over everyone else, this was our way to leave the bloody past behind, our never again. We were told to cleanse ourselves from the taint of what injustice did to us, and we thought it meant to stand up for ourselves alone, to claim our place, to wave our flag, to make our little ark, to build a homeland of our own, and close the borders — that's the way it's done.

So we didn't make it to the promised land, and we weren't the only ones. Oh, no. We saw them across the canyons, on the bluffs, down the valley, walking in circles just like us, looking for the small way in, losing our ways, trying to find the river's edge, the green mirage that always melted away.

And the ancestor who hides said: Trust no one. We only carry seed for a single field, so keep it concealed.

And the ancestor who runs said: Let's move along, walk faster, cover the ground. All those others would only slow us down.

And the ancestor who builds said: Our tents are our country. We are becoming who we need to be, to build that other home. Then we can learn to keep borders of our own.

And the ancestor who confronts said: Fight whoever is in our way. This the only way to win our place. Anyone who tries to stop us wears Pharaoh's face.

But as we lay under the stars, we heard the wailing of their flutes, and slowly the ache of captivity began to heal. We remembered the women who washed their clothing in the river where we washed our own, how all our backs bent together, to pull the blocks of stone, how we sang in different languages to ease our pain, how the words were different, and the melodies, but the song was the same.

As we remembered, as we wept, as we became accustomed to walking free, slowly the faces of those other travelers began to change, we saw their thirst and weariness, their laughing eyes, their calloused hands. Began to wonder, what are their names? How did we forget them? How did we break apart? We heard how their drumming in the night echoed the beating of their hearts.

Step by step we learned to braid our paths, to trade our stories round the fire. Sometimes we help each other over stones, share water when we find it, handfuls of oasis dates. And sometimes we feel the clutching at our hearts, grow fearful and angry, forget each other and betray.

We sing solidarity together, but we have our doubts. If we're one for all, will the all really be for one?

Everyone chants:

It is we who plow the deserts; fill the armies they command,
load the trucks and type the memos, harvest crops across the land.
Now we stand outcast and starving, while the budget cuts expand.

But does our union make us strong enough?

It is we who wash the dishes, cook the soup and fold the shirts,
care for other people's babies, patch up everybody's hurts.
Though your lives depend upon us, still you treat us all like dirt.

But when the going gets tough, will the tough stick around?

But we're making progress now. We see the river far ahead and though
we falter, still, we take each other's hands. At last we know we'll get there,
though the going's slow. We practice every day how we'll ford the flood,
hands around wrists, making a rope from bank to bank, a kinship deeper and
more true than blood. What makes us chosen is that we choose each other,
moving at the speed of trust, together.

The one who hides carries the seeds and scrolls for all. The one who runs
runs ahead to scout the way. The one who builds is organizing teams. The
one who fights is fighting for collective dreams. We still lie down among the
stones and thorns, but we smell the milk and honey on the breeze.

RED SEA

Originally written in April 2002,
but painfully relevant in the fall of 2023.

This Passover, who reclines?
Only the dead, their cupped hands filling slowly
with the red wine of war. We are not free.
The blood on the doorposts does not protect anyone.

They say that other country over there
dim blue in the twilight
farther than the orange stars exploding over our roofs
is called peace.

The bread of affliction snaps in our hands like bones,
is dust in our mouths. This bitterness brings tears to our eyes.
The figs and apples are sour. We have many more
than four questions. We dip and dip,
salt stinging our fingers.
Unbearable griefs braided into a rope so tight
we can hardly breathe,
whether we bless or curse,
this is captivity.
We would cross the water if we knew how.
Everyone blames everyone else for barring the way.

Listen, they say there is honey swelling in golden combs, over there,
dates as sweet and brown as lovers' cheekbones,
bread as fragrant as rest,
but the turbulent water will not part for us.
We've lost the trick of it.

Back then, one man's faith opened the way.
He stepped in, we were released, our enemies drowned.

This time we're tied at the ankles.
We cannot cross until we carry each other,
all of us refugees, all of us prophets.
No more taking turns on history's wheel,
trying to collect old debts no one can pay.
The sea will not open that way.

This time that country
is what we promise each other,
our rage pressed cheek to cheek
until tears flood the space between,
until there are no enemies left,
because this time no one will be left to drown
and all of us must be chosen.
This time it's all of us or none.

TISHA B'AV

There is a crack, a crack in everything.
That's how the light gets in.

Leonard Cohen, "Anthem"

I will not weep for shattered eggshells from which birdsong fills the world.

I will not weep for seed pods split apart to fling their airy parachutes into the wind.

I will not weep for chrysalides, crucibles of unmaking from which we come like flowers from buds, made new.

My wings have opened. I will not crouch here crying over dead skin. I will follow the scent of honey to the beckoning blossoms that dust my flight with gold.

Why would I cry over temples destroyed when we are all the temple we need?

I will grind eggshell into efun, ancestral powder of protection.

I will tend the milkweed that the wind brings to my garden and feed the pollinators of the world to come.

I will keep dissolving what no longer serves, be a cauldron of the imaginal, let the broken reinvent itself into dazzling form.

Come, let us leave this ancient dust, these stones that once contained eternal light. Can you not feel it shining in our bones?

Infinite Tribe

HANNAH'S SHAWL

Blessed is blessing,
and praise be to praise.
My heart rejoices and I am made strong
as the vine that winds around a broken trunk
and reaches beyond its shattering
from earth to the stars.

All the powers of the mighty may be overthrown
and the anguish of the downtrodden
vanish like mist, the poor be raised from the ashes,
the hungry fed and the arrogant brought low,
for no one, in the end, prevails by force, not even
the strongman with his thugs, and not
by our railing against our lot, fists raised,
shouting our lonely outrage into the dark.
Open your eyes! We are not alone. That
is the magic.

I have wrapped myself in this shawl
woven from my own desire, from the love
of all things intertwined, from the opposite
of alone. My shawl is made of the gratitude
of rain-washed trees, and the shiver
of dry wind turning sweat to salt on my skin,
of how flocks of birds

migrate willy-nilly across the heavens
drawn by a wordless longing.
So I have called from the depths of my being
for a fertile life, and been answered.

My shawl is of the multitudes,
a call and response between toad and constellation,
mayfly and ocean swell, microbe and tectonic plate,

you, dear one, in your distant city and century,
and the flicker of candlelight
shining in my cup of tea,

for prayer is knit from the bindings
between everything that lives,
for you may pull my shawl around you
plucked out of all the noisy truth of your life
and wrap yourself in the
still and trembling heart of the web
and my prayer, the prayer
of a faithful and childless woman
crying out her heart endless generations ago
is the mother of all our prayers.

PSALM 23

If I were a sheep, this earth would shepherd me
and I should not want.
If I were a skylark the sky would lift me high
and I should not fall.
I lie down in the greenest of pastures
cradled in the scent of growing leaves.
I am held in the tumult of the rapids
until I come to still waters
for the true spirit that is in me
is met
in the wild generosity
of the living, untamed world.
It meets me in your smiling eyes,
and in your blazing indignation.

When my soul grows weary I am restored
as sap rising in spring restores the trees,
because we are together,
and because I am made of spirit and earth
and so are you, and the sheep, the lark, the tree, the grass
I am called, tugged, by our entangled rootings
back onto the paths of righteousness.

Even when I am walking in those valleys
that are shadowed by death
without horizon or compass
where I feel most alone and wrong and confused
I will fear no harm. Because you are with me
and I am with you,
there is always a rod like a shaft of light.
There is forever a staff like the shoulder of a friend.
There is navigation in the dark.

Even when I am surrounded by ill intent,
when danger glints in the shadows

and hatred snarls and snaps at my heels,
there is a feast of joy spread before me.
I am anointed as if with sacred oils.
I am veiled in the grace
of being alive, here, now, myself,
with you. My cup is never empty.
It brims over and waters the gardens
of the troubled world.

For there is goodness and mercy enough
for everyone, for all of the days of our lives,
and it is in our hands to plant the seeds of it
in every place on earth, and even among the stars,
so we may dwell in the house of love forever.

THE BURNING BUSH

A million burning bushes demand of us
that we become prophets
that we all walk, stammering,
into what we don't yet know we can do.
There is no narrower place than this.
It is the bondage of things.

We can't stand trembling
at the crumbling cliff's edge.
We must walk down into this boiling sea
choked with sargassum
as it climbs past every high tide line
toward our old lives that are stacked
like empty boxes along the shore,
and open a way.

Of all the useless merchandise
in this cluttered world
despair is the luxury
we can least afford.

A million burning souls
speak from the smoke and flame
and are not consumed
saying now, now is the moment
to be ablaze.

ASHERAH, TREE OF LIFE

My lungs hold branches upside down:
Bronchia and leafy crown
I from egg and thou from seed
Each gives what the other needs
I am breathing tree
Tree is breathing me.

Barbara McAfee, "Breathing Trees"

She came to me as roble
scattering pink flowers
from slender limbs
and she came as flamboyán
all feather and flame
and ceiba, with muscular, buttressed roots
and cotton silk drifting from brown pods.
She said, do not be reluctant to bloom,
come what may.

Once she unfurled her tender green
beside weathered stone
and was the consort of God,
a pillar in every garden,
a sacred grove to those who come,
and her pathways all of peace

until the singular jealous masculine lord of men cried out
you shall have no others before me
banished her resplendent manyness
and made her fistfuls of winged seeds
heresies in the wind.

Hewn down to the bare root
she is always springing back to life
all around us. She is the mangrove,

building islands in the waves
where branches drip roots
and green herons nest in her arms.

She is always springing back,
the leaf-carved stone in the corner,
the new growth poking up
from charred stumps,
yagrumo, guardian of the forest,
the first to shoot skyward from ruin.

She has always been here,
she is sumac burning red at dusk,
a wind bent cypress crone,
light sifting through coast redwoods
their vast stillness, their fronds of hair,
the prehistoric tree ferns
with their fractal plumes.

O carpet of roots and fungal thread, we chant,
o tree of life, spread above us
your rain forest canopies
that make the rivers of the sky,
prickle us awake
with your saguaro skin,
quench our thirst
with your reservoirs of sap,
fill our scorched lungs
with the sweetness of your breath,
for you are the dawn of all breathing.
You bring rain to settle our dust
and lend us dappled shade
when the sky is blistering.
Teach us to keep rising.

Around you spin the blades of saws.
Around you the steel jaws of bulldozers

tear at the roots of being and break bones.
Around you, arsonists pour gasoline on tinder.
You do not smite. You don't avenge.
You fall, disintegrate, swell
with improbable buds, and leaf out
again.

We will fill our fists with peach pits,
with pine cones, with silvery seed
to plant between our ribs,
for when they buried us they didn't know
how we would spring back
how we would branch out,
how fire makes us germinate.

Tree of life, mother of abundance, she who returns,
teach us to sprout new life from every scar
and offer ourselves to the bees.
Teach us to be groves to all who come,
and let our pathways be of peace.

EDO'S SONG

When we walked out of the city gates,
away from the walls of Sodom
we were given a test: *don't look back*
he said. Forget everything within
those walls, forget your pleasure,
walking among the market stalls,
how you cradled your babies
to your breasts, their milky smell,
the neighbors calling to each other
across the lines of laundry in the wind.
All of that is doomed.
We are leaving. Don't look back.

But I had daughters.

See me, then,
how my left arm reached behind me,
then everything followed that
gesture of longing,
into the slow pivot of my body
back toward what I loved

and the crackle of cells gone crystalline,
my hair into salty seaweed, rock salt
my bones, those fingers, all aglitter
still reaching.

The fearful call it punishment.
Lot's wife, they say, forgetting
I had a name.

But I was flesh made covenant,
salt that binds us to our words,
and to each other.

Oh, you can't imagine!
I was love made mineral,
an archive of memory
against the spoilage of the times.
Don't be afraid.
It's easy to make the salty choice.
Turn back and face the fallen.
Remember loving them.
Say their names.

KADDISH FOR MY COMMUNIST FATHER

Joyously celebrated be the infinite complexity and beauty of the universe, its endless dialectic, its loops of positive and negative feedback, equilibrium and change, its constant evolution; and celebrated be human creativity and solidarity and courage. May they establish liberation in our lifetimes and in our days and in the lives of all peoples everywhere, speedily and soon, and let us say ¡Que viva!

Praise to the great dialectic of change always unfolding possibilities.

May the deep wells of humanity and hope within us gush forth into the world and may there be principled unity and immense and powerful coalitions, clearheaded analysis and breathtaking vision, and practical, hard work done together with joy. May the local and the global embrace, may the personal and political embrace, may intellect, emotion and flesh dance together. May our deepest desire for connection dissolve all factions and wash away all unnecessary conflict. Blessed and praised be solidarity, extolled and honored beyond all the songs and chants, manifestos and movements that have ever been crafted, for it is our greatest hope and we must cultivate it in all we do, and let us say ¡Que viva!

May all who are bound up in the toils of greed for power and wealth, and all who are trapped in the fear of scarcity, in selfish individualism and the short term strategies of desperation, and all who are confused by privilege and wounded by the ruthless heartlessness of oppression, be released to join in the common good of us all which is far greater than any other reward.

May liberation arise abundant and universal from our own hands and hearts and minds; may there be peace and justice and life for us, and for all beings, and let us say ¡Que viva!

May we whose love and labor bring life-giving food forth from soil and waters and cooking pots create a world that is sustaining and sustainable for ourselves and for all that lives, and let us say ¡Que viva!

RACIAL JUSTICE INVOCATION

This piece was written for Kehilla Community Synagogue in Piedmont, California and shared on Kol Nidre 5779/2018.

In the heart of this congregation, we have planted the seeds of racial justice, a handful of grains in the earth of our belief, a place to tell untold stories, a place to draw maps of long journeys, a place to unveil our heartbreaks and look our ignorances in the face. The seeds are only beginnings, possibilities that must be watered, weeded, fed. It means we have to haul buckets, spread manure, and pull up the wickedly thorned thistles of our defenses. It means getting down and dirty. This racial justice initiative is a not-yet sprouted garden of unequaled beauty germinating among us, medicinal, nourishing, fragrant, and the seeds begin in conversation, in a cluster of six bare earth plots called affinity groups. There are trowels enough to go around, and each one of you has a place to sit cross-legged on the ground and begin.

Or to change the poem, in the heart of this congregation there is a new song that we can all dance to, and this is its choreography.

We who have hovered at the edges, with our bundles of silence, our cracked rage, our suitcases full of dispossession, our not rocking the boat for fear of drowning, our letting our white cousins massacre our names, our letting our white cousins ask if we are the help, aching to be known, aching to speak our Jewishness in accents you have never heard before, we who are called Indigenous, called Black and of color, we Jews beyond the Ashkenazi pale, will step, hobble, roll into the center, unassimilated, fiercely lovely in our unedited truths, bringing all our ancestors speaking all their languages into this room, saying we are not confusing, singing we Jews are a garment of a thousand threads, a coat of twenty million colors, for the heart of the Jewish world lives equally in every Jew, and no one is exotic, and every one of us is Jewish enough, and however we travel through the world is a Jewish path.

We who have held the center, raised the roof beams, wrestled old words into new melodies, carried our treasured scraps of Yiddishkeit next to our hearts, carried our shtetls, our Europe, our ship's passenger lists, our landings in the goldeneh medina, we who walked unknowing into the occupation of other people's worlds, walked unknowing into whiteness that coated us bit by bit like layers of shellac, deadening our senses, we who are etched with the pain of separation from all our others, we settlers hungry for unsettling, we will step, hobble, roll outward to the rim of the circle and hold space for our kin, will fast from speaking first, will fast from being the ones who know, will feast on listening, will let the varnish crack and peel, saying we will not be confused, singing the heart of the Jewish world lives equally in every Jew, and no one is the norm, and every one of us is a real Jew, and traveling together through the world is our Jewish path. And stepping in and stepping out we will weave a dance of justice right here in this room.

There are dance shoes enough to go around, and each one of you has a place to tap your feet, warm up your muscles and move, a place called affinity group. Indigenous people, we have a place. Black people and people of color, we have a place. Mizrahim and Sephardim, we have a place. People with white privilege, we have a place. White parents of children of color, we have a place. Families of color including white co-parents, we have a place. One two three, one two three, dance!

AXXESS

Recite the name of each accommodation
as if it had come down the mountain
clasped in a prophet's arms.
Remember we are commanded
to make walls fall down.

Open each padlocked gate
each barrier of noise
each barricade of scent
as if it was the ark
and each of us was torah,
unfurling in the dark.

It could take all the holy day
to make it right. All night
while the agenda waits.
It could take us all our lives
to understand the meaning of
no more spoons left, only knives.

This is the work, this asking,
listening, this opening the door
after door after door. This,
not the thing that comes after,
but the thing that comes before.

Ingathering each irreplaceable
unique and lovely one of us.
Slowing the whole thing down
until there is nothing left
but common ground.

MADE OF

We are made of the mineral dust of stars and every molecule of us burns with the memory of vastness and splendor. We are living constellations, minute fiery suns, each of us with our orbiting miraculous worlds, our silent moons, all born from the hunger of atoms to embrace. Our light reaches beyond us, through the beautiful dark, through the universe without end. Everything that exists, has existed, will ever exist in all the unimaginable folded flower of time is holy, and there is nothing ever and anywhere that is not Spirit.

We are made of earth, small seeds, dreams of photosynthesis, curled inside brown husks, made to crack painfully from our shells, to push heavy soil aside, to move, stubborn and fragile toward our destinies, into sun and rain. To break and grow green, break and flower, to be trees of life, and fall broken onto the ground becoming rich humus full green unbroken dreams. Everything that is, we turn into ourselves and give back as soil. Give back as oxygen. What we breathe is each other. Nothing that lives is alone.

We are made of water: salty rivers run in our veins, lymph ebbs and swells, saliva and tears leak into the air and dry. We are always changing: wide seas into clouds, rain into puddles, rivers into muddy fields that run along ditches into the sea. We flow, freeze, boil, rise, disperse, are hurled this way and that. We declare that we are the blue edge of glaciers, the great ocean swell, stagnant teeming ponds, months long tropical downpours, the delicate tracery of frost on a dry leaf, rusty drip of a faucet. We are the shape of what's happened to us. We are caught up in doing, and whirl through our lives, suffering, joyful, filled with doubt. And yet we return to ourselves again and again, to the Self that is all there is. We are made of water, called to find our true level by that great force of love we call gravity. We are made to trust our destination. We are not lost.

Olivia Levins Holden

WINGS

Cuba y Puerto Rico son　　*Cuba and Puerto Rico*
de un pájaro las dos alas,　*are the two wings of one bird,*
reciben flores o balas　　*receiving flowers or bullets*
sobre el mismo corazón.　*into the same heart.*

Lola Rodríguez de Tió

Two wings of one bird said the exiled poet
whose words burned too many holes of truth
through the colonial air of a different iron-toothed occupation.
Nothing divides the suffering of the conquered.
Two wings, she said, *of a single bird, with one heart between them,*
taking bullets and roses, soldiers and prison bars and poetry,
into one pulse of protest. One bird she insisted
as the ship pulled away from San Juan headed for Havana, 1879.

A century later we are still the wounded wing,
fluttering, dragged through the waves, the next empire
plucking feathers from living flesh. *White egret within the foam,*
cried another poet, returning after long years in the dry solitude of Spain:
garza, garza blanca. Those ruffled reefs are infested now
with unexploded bombs. Pastures where white birds
still grace the backs of cattle, are dusted with the toxic waste
of rehearsal for invasion, that seeps into the blood of children,
so that cancer is a required course in the high schools of Vieques,
giving a whole new meaning to the term "drop out."
I was born into an occupied country. I am that wing.

What kind of Jew are you, receiving bullets and roses
as if in a Palestinian heart?
I am the Jewish great-great-granddaughter of Puerto Rican slaveholders.
I am the Puerto Rican great-great-granddaughter of Ukrainian socialists.
I am the surviving branch of a family tree split at the turn of the last century
holding the photograph of nameless cousins

who missed the last train to Siberia
and fell into the trenches of summer
as Nazi armies rolled across the farmlands of Kherson.
I am the educated granddaughter of a Puerto Rican seamstress
who never went past the eighth grade,
whose fingers bled into the spandex of sweatshop assembly line girdles,
a long subway ride from the barrios where she lived, the granddaughter
of an electrician wiring battleships in the Brooklyn Navy Yard,
of a communist studying law at night
and serving deli by day, and of a social worker
trying to plug the holes in immigrant lifeboats.
I am a daughter of occupation and conquest, of deportation and escape.
I am a daughter of people who were outgunned and refused to die.
I am a colonial subject with a stone in my hand when I listen to the news.
I am a fierce Latina Jew holding out a rose to Palestine.

I am the Jewish grand-niece of a Puerto Rican WWII soldier
cracking up in the bloody Pacific,
in the service of an army that always sent the brown men in first.
I am the Puerto Rican cousin
of Jewish evacuees trying to flee eastward, shot in the back
by Ukrainian collaborators who lived just down the road.
I am the daughter of red pacifists married in the year of Korea,
a two-winged child conceived as the Rosenbergs died, born as Lolita
was shackled into her quarter century of punishment
for shooting into the air.
I was born Jewish in an occupied Caribbean land, speaking Spanish
with the accent of escaped slaves and hungry coffee laborers,
because my great-grandfather would not fight Japan for the Tsar,
because he evaded yet another imperial draft,
and washed up in New York City
where barrio meets shtetl, girl meets boy and solidarity was my lullaby.

What kind of independentista are you, to weep for Israeli soldiers
drafted into accepting atrocity as a fact of life,
beating out the ritmo of kaddish for colonialists killed in rightful revolution
on the conga of your caribe heart?

I am the proud cousin of a banned Boricua writer climbing out of his deathbed
to raise the flag of Puerto Rico on the third anniversary of the US invasion,
just two weeks before he died of TB
contracted in the bitter prison cells of Valladolid.
I am a distant relative of the first woman of Puerto Rico burned
by the Inquisition, in the name of Christ,
for being a secret Jew. I am the descendant of hacendados
who worked their own slave children to the bone in tobacco fields ripening
over the traces of uprooted plantings of casabe
and of the pale brown daughters of dark women,
taken into the marriage beds of landholding men,
criada servants deemed good enough for younger sons,
setting their wide cheeks and mouths into their children's bones.

I am the descendant of invaders and invaded,
now riding high on history's wheel, now crushed below,
of those evicted and their village burned,
of those who rode the horses and set the flames.

What kind of song is this? Whose side are you on?
Two wings, I say with the exiled poets of my country
to my dispossessed and dispossessing cousins
in the land it seems that everyone was promised.
Two wings with a single heart between them:
intifada and partisaner, refusenik and cimarron.
Nothing divides the suffering. One bird full of bullets and roses,
one bird with its wounded pinions,
one heart that if it breaks is broken. I *know* there are two bloody wings,
but it is one bird trying to lift itself into the air,
one bird turning in circles on the ground, because
two wings rising and falling together
is the forgotten principle of flight. Two wings
torn by tempestuous weather.
One bird struggling into the light.

Prophecy

V'AHAVTA

Say these words when you lie down and when you rise up,
when you go out and when you return. In times of mourning
and in times of joy. Inscribe them on your doorposts,
embroider them on your garments, tattoo them on your shoulders,
teach them to your children, your neighbors, your enemies,
recite them in your sleep, here in the cruel shadow of empire:
Another world is possible.

Thus spoke the prophet Roque Dalton:
All together they have more death than we,
but all together, we have more life than they.
There is more bloody death in their hands
than we could ever wield, unless
we lay down our souls to become them,
and then we will lose everything. So instead,

imagine winning. This is your sacred task.
This is your power. Imagine
every detail of winning, the exact smell of the summer streets
in which no one has been shot, the muscles you have never
unclenched from worry, gone soft as newborn skin,
the sparkling taste of food when we know
that no one on earth is hungry, that the beggars are fed,
that the old man under the bridge and the woman
wrapping herself in thin sheets in the back seat of a car,
and the children who suck on stones,
nest under a flock of roofs that keep multiplying their shelter.
Lean with all your being towards that day
when the poor of the world shake down a rain of good fortune
out of the heavy clouds, and justice rolls down like waters.

Defend the world in which we win as if it were your child.
It is your child.
Defend it as if it were your lover.
It is your lover.

When you inhale and when you exhale
breathe the possibility of another world
into the 37.2 trillion cells of your body
until it shines with hope.
Then imagine more.

Imagine rape is unimaginable. Imagine war is a scarcely credible rumor
that the crimes of our age, the grotesque inhumanities of greed,
the sheer and astounding shamelessness of it, the vast fortunes
made by stealing lives, the horrible normalcy it came to have,
is unimaginable to our heirs, the generations of the free.

Don't waver. Don't let despair sink its sharp teeth
into the throat with which you sing. Escalate your dreams.
Make them burn so fiercely that you can follow them down
any dark alleyway of history and not lose your way.
Make them burn clear as a starry drinking gourd
over the grim fog of exhaustion, and keep walking.

Hold hands. Share water. Keep imagining.
So that we, and the children of our children's children
may live.

SUMMONS

Last night I dreamed
ten thousand grandmothers
from the twelve hundred corners of the earth
walked out into the gap
one breath deep
between the bullet and the flesh
between the bomb and the family.

They told me we cannot wait for governments.
There are no peacekeepers boarding planes.
There are no leaders who dare to say
every life is precious, so it will have to be us.

They said we will cup our hands around each heart.
We will sing the earth's song, the song of water,
a song so beautiful that vengeance will turn to weeping,
the mourners will embrace, and grief replace
every impulse toward harm.

Ten thousand is not enough, they said,
so we have sent this dream, like a flock of doves
into the sleep of the world. Wake up. Put on your shoes.

You who are reading this, I am bringing bandages
and a bag of scented guavas from my trees. I think
I remember the tune. Meet me at the corner.
Let's go.

RECIPROCITY

Fifteen thousand generations ago our ancestors dreamt us, dreamt this unimaginable moment of the world, held the small seeds of us in the curved palms of their newly human hands and breathed on the possibility of who we would become. They sat in circles around fire, telling each other about their long descended children who would be born in our time, and walk through the great peril of the planet to the other side. They could not picture us, so they covered the walls of their caves with the prints of their own hands. Five thousand generations ago they began carving patterns into the shells of ostrich eggs and made words to teach their art. They left us messages about water and sky, earth and animals. Sucking on the marrows of roasted antelope bones, they spoke of us softly, remembering the distant future moment in which we are gathered in this ceremony. In which we speak of them, hold in our curved palms the gift of their dreams and seeds and fires, from which we have come, step by step across the years. We are the fulfillment of those ancient dreams, they tell us. We are enough.

And we who are gathered now, today, are the ancestors of dreams that others will fulfill. Children so distantly unborn that we cannot imagine their faces turn toward us as to an ancient fire. We offer them our love and trouble, our hopes and fears, everything we have gathered, everything we know, these ritual words in languages that will have vanished, and we tell them, all that we are, we give to you, for the world you will be making, for the great mending that will be your inheritance. For you we have labored, for you we have fought and planted. For you we sing. With our breath we bless the seeds of that livable future we conjure for them, and tell them, across the uncountable years, you are all that we hoped you would be. We are proud of your unimaginable becoming. You are enough.

Ayeola Omolara Kaplan

References ❧

Cohen, Leonard. "Anthem." *The Future*. Columbia Records, 1992.

Guillén, Nicolás. "¿Puedes?" Poeticous blog, www.poeticous.com/guillen
/puedes. Translation by Aurora Levins Morales.

McAfee, Barbara. "Breathing Trees." *World of Wonders*. Big Bug Music, 2013.

Rich, Adrienne. "Song." *Diving into the Wreck: Poems 1971–1972* (New York:
W. W. Norton & Company, 2013), 20.

Rodríguez de Tió, Lola. "A Cuba." *Mi Libro de Cuba: Poesías* (Habana:
Imprenta La Moderna, 1893), 3–6. Translation by Aurora Levins Morales.

About the Artists &

JUANA ALICIA

Born in 1953, Juana Alicia had many rich cultural influences growing up in Detroit, near Diego Rivera's Industry murals, in a Spanish and Yiddish-speaking household within a majority Black neighborhood. In her teens and early 20's, she was swept up by the Chicanx Movement, particularly the United Farm Workers struggle. She was recruited by Cesar Chavez to work with the union in Salinas, which she did from 1971–76. This was key to her education as an artist and activist. She has worked as a muralist, printmaker, sculptor, illustrator, and studio painter since then. She worked for forty years as an educator: elementary, migrant, and bilingual education, in arts academies and universities, before retiring seven years ago to dedicate herself full-time to her artwork. Her experience as a mother and a grandmother has also informed and given greater meaning to her artistic production.

Her style, akin to genres of contemporary Latin American literary movements, can be characterized as magical and social realism, and her work is frequently inspired by literature.

She has moved back and forth across the US-Mexico border for many years, and since 2006, has resided part-time in Mérida, Yucatán, and in Berkeley, California. She has created murals in both places, and her binational experience has inspired the project which she is currently completing with her co-author and husband, Tirso González Araiza: to illustrate the Yucatec Mayan folk tale, LA X'TABAY, which will be exhibited this summer at the San Francisco Arts Commission Gallery and in the fall at the Museum of Anthropology in Mérida. Working in both countries has enabled her to form connections and create projects with artists, environmental activists, feminists and Indigenous communities in Mexico and the United States.

ROAN BOUCHER

Roan is a trans disabled Jewish artist, parent, and facilitator. In 2010 he co-founded the Anti-Oppression Resource and Training Alliance (AORTA), a worker co-op of facilitators and strategists supporting movement organizations. He makes art about movements, queers, Judaism, and liberation. He is rooted in the Southeast, on Eno, Tutelo, Saponi, Occaneechi, Shakori, and Tuscarora land.

LAURYL BERGER-CHUN

To learn more about Lauryl's art you can write to Laurylbc@gmail.com.

OLIVIA LEVINS HOLDEN

Olivia (she/they) is a queer, mixed Boricua muralist, organizer, artist, and educator living on Dakota homeland, Mni Sota Makoce, Minneapolis, Minnesota. Olivia's work explores many ways that the arts can transform and support movements, tell stories, plant seeds, and combat toxic narratives. They center processes of community involvement and collective design, drawing from conversations and people's history to create collaborative murals and public art, believing that the process is as essential as the final artwork. Since 2009, they have created and led the creation of murals in Minneapolis, California, and Puerto Rico, including Minneapolis murals *Waves of Change/Oleadas de Cambio* (2015), *Defend, Nurture, Grown Phillips* (2019), *Wiidookodaadiwag/They Help Each Other* (2019), and *Ritmos y Raices de Resistencia* (2021). With her artist collective, Studio Thalo, Olivia creates live-painted mobile murals to reflect conversations and events.

Olivia is a 2022 McKnight Fellow for Community Engaged Artists, was a 2015 recipient of the Forecast Public Art project grant and has served as a facilitator and mentor for project-based learning through programs such as Comunidades Latinas Unidas En Servicio (CLUES), Latinx Muralism Apprenticeship, Studio 400, and is a founding member of the Creatives After Curfew collective. She serves as the Art of Radical Collaboration (ARC) Manager at Hope Community, Inc where she has trained artists and led community murals with youth and adults through the Power of Vision (POV) Mural project since 2017 and facilitates the Transformational Creative Strategies Training (TRCSTR). She has a BA in History from Smith College.

AYEOLA OMOLARA KAPLAN

Ayeola is a Black and queer Atlanta-based pop-surrealist painter. Through depicting the intersections of identity, class, and spirituality, she hopes to contribute to the moving canon of revolutionary art. She creates with the belief that art can be weaponized as self-defense against an anti-truth culture plagued by unhealed generational trauma. Her work features empowering and electrifying imagery created to energize people, as well as celebrate marginalized folks carrying themselves with clout. The pieces exist as spiritual tools created with the intention to manifest a blissful and equitable future.

RICARDO LEVINS MORALES

Ricardo is an artsist and social justice warrior/healer. He is from Maricao, Puerto Rico and works out of a storefront studio in Minneapolis in the US. He is closely connected with artists, activists and organizers throughout the social justice ecosystem.

Website: www.rlmartstudio.com

WENDY ELISHEVA SOMERSON

Wendy is a non-binary white Ashkenazi Jewish somatic healer, writer, visual artist, and activist who helped found the Seattle chapter of Jewish Voice for Peace. They facilitate Ruach, body-based Jewish healing groups held in an anti-Zionist, anti-racist, and feminist framework.

Instagram: @wendyelisheva
Website: www.etsy.com/shop/CorvidCrossingStudio

ARIELLE TONKIN

Arielle is a queer, mixed Moroccan and Ashkenazi Jewish artist, educator, and spiritual director working to dismantle white supremacy through arts & culture work and Jewish and interfaith education work. Arielle weaves relationships and materializes conversations: the Muslim-Jewish Arts Fellowship, Arts Jam for Social Change, Tzedek Lab, SVARA and Inside Out Wisdom in Action are among their networks of accountability, collective power, creative collaboration and care. Arielle's artwork and social practice presences, queers, and formalizes the belief that healing through relationship can shift the fabric of social space and eventually, one braided thread at a time, shift the structure of the physical world.

About Aurora Levins Morales &

Aurora Levins Morales is a cuir Ashkenazi Boricua writer of poetry, essays, and fiction. A child of blacklisted communist parents, she grew up immersed in social justice movements and the poetry of liberation, and came into public voice as part of the collective eruptions of radical art of the 1970s and '80s. She is the author of nine books, including *Medicine Stories, Kindling, Remedios,* and *Silt.* Her poetry is widely used in synagogues and churches, in schools and at rallies, painted on walls and recited at weddings, translated into seven languages and reprinted in dozens of anthologies. After forty years in the San Francisco Bay Area, she now lives at Finca la Lluvia, an agro-poetry project in the western mountains of Boriken, also known as Puerto Rico. *The Story of What Is Broken Is Whole: An Aurora Levins Morales Reader* will be published in 2024 by Duke University Press. Find her on Patreon and at www.auroralevinsmorales.com.

How to Support Aurora &

Aurora Levins Morales is a community supported artist and movement elder, without salary, benefits or a pension. You can support her work, read unpublished pieces and updates on her work, and communicate with her at www.patreon.com/auroralevinsmorales.

Other Books by Aurora &

BOOKS BY AURORA

Getting Home Alive, with Rosario Morales

Remedios: Stories of Earth and Iron from the History of Puertorriqueñas

Kindling: Writings On the Body

Cosecha and Other Stories, with Rosario Morales

Medicine Stories: Essays for Radicals

Silt: Prose Poems

ANTHOLOGIES FEATURING AURORA

This Bridge Called My Back: Writings by Radical Women of Color

Telling to Live: Latina Feminist Testimonios

Women Writing Resistance: Essays on Latin America and the Caribbean

Palabrera Press is a self-publishing venture
by Aurora Levins Morales.

Ayin Press is an artist-run publishing platform
and production studio rooted in Jewish culture
and emanating outward.

Both online and in print, we seek to celebrate
artists and thinkers at the margins and explore
the growing edges of collective consciousness
through a diverse range of mediums and genres.

Ayin was founded on a deep belief in the power of
culture and creativity to heal, transform, and up-
lift the world we share and build together. We are
committed to amplifying a polyphony of voices
from within and beyond the Jewish world.

For more information about our current or
upcoming projects and titles, reach out to us at
info@ayinpress.org. To make a tax-deductible
contribution to our work, visit our website at
www.ayinpress.org/donate.